GoLive™ Keyboard Shortcuts for Mac OS

Keep this handy list of shortcuts close to your keyboard for quick reference

File Menu	Option+F	Header|Header 4	Shft+Option+Command+4
New	Command+N	Header|Header 5	Shft+Option+Command+5
New Site|Blank	Option+Command+N	Header|Header 6	Shft+Option+Command+6
New Site|Import from Folder	Option+Command+O	Alignment|Left	Shift+Command+G
Open	Command+O	Alignment|Center	Shift+Command+M
Close	Command+W	Alignment|Right	Shift+Command+R
Save	Command+S	List|Default Unnumbered List	Command+U
Save As	Shift+Command+S		
Revert to Saved	Option+Command+Z	**Special Menu**	Option+P
FTP Browser	Shift+Command+F	New Link	Command+L
WebDAV Browser	Shift+Command+W	Remove Link	Option+Command+L
Page Setup	Shift+Command+P	Add to Keywords	Command+K
Print	Command+P	Start Tabluator Indexing	Command+Option+T
Exit	Command+Q	Show in Default Browser	Command+T
Edit Menu	Option+E	Check Syntax	Option+Command+K
Undo	Command+Z	Use Macro	Command+M
Redo	Shift+Command+Z	New Element	Shift+Option+Command+E
Cut	Command+X	New Text	Shift+Option+Command+T
Copy	Command+C	New Comment	Shift+Option+Command+C
Paste	Command+V	New Generic Element	Shift+Option+Command+G
Select All	Command+A	New Attribute	Shift+Option+Command+A
Duplicate	Command+D	Toggle Binary	Shift+Option+Command+B
Find	Command+F	Document Statistic	Shift+Option+Command+I
Find Next	Command+G	**Site Menu**	Option+S
Find Selection	Command+H	Update/Rescan	F5
Replace	Command+R	Settings	Option+Command+Y
Replace & Find Next	Option+Command+R	**Design Menu**	Option+D
Check Spelling	Option+Command+U	**Movie Menu**	Option+M
Hide Invisible Items	Command+I	**Window Menu**	Option+W
Show Link Warnings	Shift+Command+L	Next	Command+F6
Web Settings	Shift+Command+Y	Previous	Shift+Command+F6
Keyboard Shortcuts	Shift+Option+Command+K	Hide Palettes	Command+J
Preferences	Command+Y	Toolbar	Command+0
Type Menu	Option+T	Objects	Command+2
Font|Edit Font Sets	Option+Command+F	Color	Command+3
Style|Plain Text	Shift+Command+N	Inspector	Command+1
Style|Bold	Shift+Command+B	View Controller	Command+9
Style|Italic	Shift+Command+I	Align	Command+8
Style|Strikeout	Shift+Command+A	Table	Command+6
Style|Teletype	Shift+Command+T	Site Navigator	Command+5
Header|None	Shft+Option+Command+0	JavaScript Shell	Command+4
Header|Header 1	Shft+Option+Command+1	History	Command+7
Header|Header 2	Shft+Option+Command+2	**Help Menu**	Option+H
Header|Header 3	Shft+Option+Command+3	GoLive Help	F1

S0-EJH-292

GoLive™ Keyboard Shortcuts for Windows

Keep this handy list of shortcuts close to your keyboard for quick reference

File Menu	Alt+F
New	Ctrl+N
New Site|Blank	Alt+Ctrl+N
New Site|Import from Folder	Alt+Ctrl+O
Open	Ctrl+O
Close	Ctrl+W
Save	Ctrl+S
Save As	Shift+Ctrl+S
Revert to Saved	Alt+Ctrl+Z
FTP Browser	Shift+Ctrl+F
WebDAV Browser	Shift+Ctrl+W
Page Setup	Shift+Ctrl+P
Print	Ctrl+P
Exit	Ctrl+Q
Edit Menu	Alt+E
Undo	Ctrl+Z
Redo	Shift+Ctrl+Z
Cut	Ctrl+X
Copy	Ctrl+C
Paste	Ctrl+V
Select All	Ctrl+A
Duplicate	Ctrl+D
Find	Ctrl+F
Find Next	Ctrl+G
Find Selection	Ctrl+H
Replace	Ctrl+R
Replace & Find Next	Alt+Ctrl+R
Check Spelling	Alt+Ctrl+U
Hide Invisible Items	Ctrl+I
Show Link Warnings	Shift+Ctrl+L
Web Settings	Shift+Ctrl+Y
Keyboard Shortcuts	Shift+Alt+Ctrl+K
Preferences	Ctrl+Y
Type Menu	Alt+T
Font|Edit Font Sets	Alt+Ctrl+F
Style|Plain Text	Shift+Ctrl+N
Style|Bold	Shift+Ctrl+B
Style|Italic	Shift+Ctrl+I
Style|Strikeout	Shift+Ctrl+A
Style|Teletype	Shift+Ctrl+T
Header|None	Shft+Alt+Ctrl+0
Header|Header 1	Shft+Alt+Ctrl+1
Header|Header 2	Shft+Alt+Ctrl+2
Header|Header 3	Shft+Alt+Ctrl+3
Header|Header 4	Shft+Alt+Ctrl+4

Header|Header 5	Shft+Alt+Ctrl+5
Header|Header 6	Shft+Alt+Ctrl+6
Alignment|Left	Shift+Ctrl+G
Alignment|Center	Shift+Ctrl+M
Alignment|Right	Shift+Ctrl+R
List|Default Unnumbered List	Ctrl+U
Special Menu	Alt+P
New Link	Ctrl+L
Remove Link	Alt+Ctrl+L
Add to Keywords	Ctrl+K
Start Tabluator Indexing	Ctrl+Alt+T
Show in Default Browser	Ctrl+T
Check Syntax	Alt+Ctrl+K
Use Macro	Ctrl+M
New Element	Shift+Alt+Ctrl+E
New Text	Shift+Alt+Ctrl+T
New Comment	Shift+Alt+Ctrl+C
New Generic Element	Shift+Alt+Ctrl+G
New Attribute	Shift+Alt+Ctrl+A
Toggle Binary	Shift+Alt+Ctrl+B
Document Statistic	Shift+Alt+Ctrl+I
Site Menu	Alt+S
Update/Rescan	F5
Settings	Alt+Ctrl+Y
Design Menu	Alt+D
Movie Menu	Alt+M
Window Menu	Alt+W
Next	Ctrl+F6
Previous	Shift+Ctrl+F6
Hide Palettes	Ctrl+J
Toolbar	Ctrl+0
Objects	Ctrl+2
Color	Ctrl+3
Inspector	Ctrl+1
View Controller	Ctrl+9
Align	Ctrl+8
Table	Ctrl+6
Site Navigator	Ctrl+5
JavaScript Shell	Ctrl+4
History	Ctrl+7
Help Menu	Alt+H
GoLive Help	F1

CORIOLIS™
Creative Professionals Press

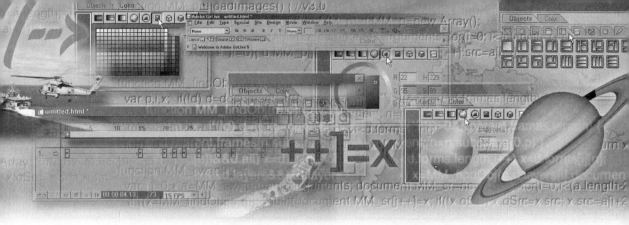

GoLive™ 5
Visual Insight

David A. Crowder

Rhonda Crowder

GoLive™ 5 Visual Insight
© 2001 The Coriolis Group. All rights reserved.

Limits of Liability and Disclaimer of Warranty
The author and publisher of this book have used their best efforts in preparing the book and the programs contained in it. These efforts include the development, research, and testing of the theories and programs to determine their effectiveness. The author and publisher make no warranty of any kind, expressed or implied, with regard to these programs or the documentation contained in this book.

The author and publisher shall not be liable in the event of incidental or consequential damages in connection with, or arising out of, the furnishing, performance, or use of the programs, associated instructions, and/or claims of productivity gains.

Trademarks
Trademarked names appear throughout this book. Rather than list the names and entities that own the trademarks or insert a trademark symbol with each mention of the trademarked name, the publisher states that it is using the names for editorial purposes only and to the benefit of the trademark owner, with no intention of infringing upon that trademark.

The Coriolis Group, LLC
14455 North Hayden Road
Suite 220
Scottsdale, Arizona 85260

(480) 483-0192
FAX: (480) 483-0193
www.coriolis.com

Library of Congress Cataloging-in-Publication Data
Crowder, David.
GoLive 5 visual insight/ by David Crowder and Rhonda Crowder.
   p. cm
   ISBN 1-57610-744-2
     1. Adobe GoLive. 2. Web sites--Design. 3. Web site development. I. Crowder, Rhonda. II. Title.
   TK5105.8885.A34 C76   2000
   005.7'2--dc21   00-047556
                    CIP

President, CEO
Keith Weiskamp

Publisher
Steve Sayre

Acquisitions Editor
Beth Kohler

Development Editor
Michelle Stroup

Product Marketing Manager
Patricia Davenport

Project Editor
Sean Tape

Technical Reviewer
Joyce Evans

Production Coordinator
Meg E. Turecek

Cover Designer
Jody Winkler

Layout Designer
April Nielsen

Printed in the United States of America
10 9 8 7 6 5 4 3 2 1

Other Titles for the Creative Professional

Looking Good on the Web
By Daniel Gray

Photoshop® 6 Visual Insight
By Ramona Pruitt and Joshua Pruitt

Adobe LiveMotion™ Visual Insight
By Molly Joss

Paint Shop Pro™ 6 Visual Insight
By Ramona Pruitt and Joshua Pruitt

QuarkXpress™ 4 In Depth
By William Harrel and Elaine Betts

Adobe PageMill® 3 f/x and Design
By Daniel Gray

Illustrator® 9 f/x and Design
By Sherry London

Painter® 6 f/x and Design
By Sherry London and Rhoda Grossman

Photoshop® 5 In Depth
By David Xenakis and Sherry London

Adobe InDesign™ f/x and Design
By Elaine Betts

To Robbie Goldstein

About the Authors

David and Rhonda Crowder have authored or coauthored nearly 20 books on computers and the Internet, including *Building a Web Site For Dummies* and the bestselling *Teach Yourself the Internet*. They were selling hypertext systems in the days when you had to explain to people what the word meant. They have been involved in the online community for over a decade and are the recipients of several awards, including *NetGuide Magazine's* Gold Site Award.

Acknowledgments

No book is ever the product of just one or two people. We owe a debt of thanks to all the many people whose hard work made this book a reality:

Michelle Stroup, Beth Kohler, Sean Tape, Paulette A. Miley, Joyce Evans, and all the other folks at Coriolis.

Kim Platt and John Kranz of Adobe.

John O. Moen of Graphic Maps (graphicmaps.com), who provided the maps used in this book, and the government agencies that supplied photographs—NASA, NOAA, the Fish and Wildlife Service, and the U.S. Navy.

Last, but never least, our agent, David Fugate, and all the other wonderful people at Waterside Productions—Maureen Maloney, Nancy Azevedo, Wendy Dietrich, and Kimberly Valentini—who keep us constantly busy and who constantly put up with us.

Contents at a Glance

Table of Contents

Introduction

About Adobe GoLive 5

GoLive began life back in 1996 as an offering from a small German software firm called go-net. This first version, called golive Pro, was only for the Macintosh platform and was only the second WYSIWYG Web page creation program for the Mac (the first was Adobe's PageMill). Although it had several promising features, the general reaction was that it was difficult to use.

Reworked as GoLive CyberStudio in early 1997 by GoLive Systems, the program began a steady progress through various releases. CyberStudio 2, released in late 1997, was already a truly sophisticated and usable program. By 1998, with the release of CyberStudio 3, a full range of Web authoring capabilities, including support for Cascading Style Sheets, made the program one of the top contenders in the Mac universe.

When Adobe acquired CyberStudio in 1999, the program came full circle, regaining its original name and knocking PageMill out of the running for good. Since that time, Adobe has kept adding more features to the program. Adobe GoLive 4 picked up the numbering where CyberStudio had left off and was the first release of the program to include a Windows version. GoLive 5 is Adobe's second release of the program.

Who Needs This Book

If you're just getting started with Web site design, this book will take you from the most basic necessities all the way through much more sophisticated techniques. You'll learn everything from simply changing fonts to adding dynamic animation to your Web pages.

More advanced users aren't neglected, either. If you're thoroughly familiar with the latest Web technologies, but need to get up to speed on GoLive, then *GoLive 5 Visual Insight* is your best route to that goal.

Visual Insight Philosophy

The Visual Insight series of books from Coriolis is geared to presenting practical knowledge in a visually appealing format that makes learning easy. Each process in the book is clearly described step by step, and each step is carefully illustrated to show exactly how to accomplish the tasks involved.

The Visual Insight books are in a two-column format, with the steps listed on the left side of the page and the accompanying figures on the right side, next to the steps they illustrate. The steps get right to the point, making sure that you waste no time in getting done what you need to get done.

This Book's Structure

This book has two parts. Part I, Techniques and Tasks, is composed of Chapters 1 through 11. This part deals with the nitty-gritty details of working with GoLive. It presents, in down-to-earth language, the precise methods and procedures you need to follow to make GoLive do what you want. Each chapter's topic is progressively more advanced, beginning with the chapter on understanding the GoLive user interface and leading up to the chapter on using Dynamic HTML to jazz up your pages.

Part II, Projects, is composed of Chapters 12 through 16. This part contains a series of projects that expand on the knowledge gained in Part I. Each project deals with how to use GoLive to solve a common, real-life Web design situation such as creating custom Web page templates, working with invisible layers, and setting the stacking order in animations.

Beginning users are probably best off starting with Chapter 1 and working their way through the book chapter by chapter. More advanced users might want to dive into the table of contents or index and go right to the areas that they need to use right away.

Part I

Techniques and Tasks

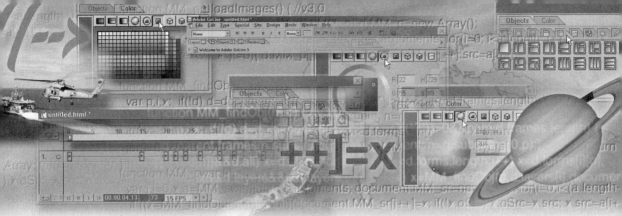

Chapter 1
The GoLive Interface

- Get to know the palettes, editors, and inspectors

- Use the different tabs of the Document Window

- Rearrange the GoLive layout to suit yourself

The Main Screen

GoLive has an attractive, well-designed interface that's meant to make creating Web pages a quick and easy task. The use of floating palette groups to present the most often used commands and adjustments is especially helpful.

Finding Your Way Around

The GoLive work area consists of a menu bar, toolbar, Document window, palettes, and Inspector.

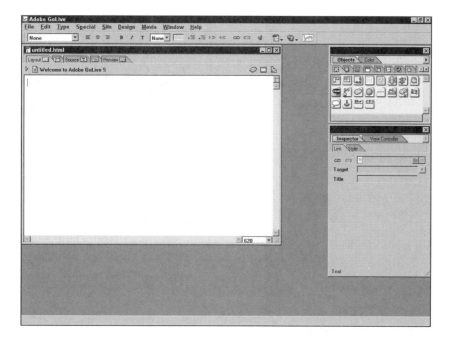

Using the Menu

The menu is the topmost element in the GoLive interface.

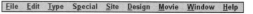

1.

Menus can be accessed either by clicking on the menu name or by pressing your Alt key and, while holding it down, pressing the key designated by the underlined letter in the menu name.

For Macs, use the Option key instead.

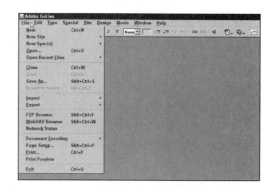

2.

Likewise, you choose a menu item by either clicking on it or, if it has an underlined letter, pressing that key (N for New, C for Close, etc.). Most menu items can also be accessed without using the menu by using a key combination. Those combinations are shown on the menu next to the item.

3.

Some menu items—those that have an arrow to their right—have a submenu from which different options may be chosen as well.

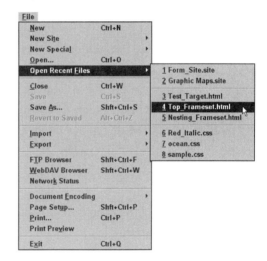

Using the Toolbar

The toolbar, which is found under the menu bar, provides a quicker and easier way to execute many commands.

Drop-down Lists and Text Boxes

Where a text box has an arrow to the right of
it, the toolbar options are presented via a drop-
down list, which is accessed by clicking on the
arrow.

*A help tip pops up when you rest the mouse pointer
on the toolbar for a moment.*

Drop-down List Options

Within the drop-down list, the options are chosen by clicking on them.

Toolbar Buttons

Most of the time, however, the toolbar presents
buttons that become three dimensional when
you rest the mouse pointer over them. The help
tip also pops up if you wait a moment. Clicking
on a button instantly executes the command.

Color Box

The color box is a different kind of toolbar
button; it launches GoLive's color options when
it is clicked on.

*See Chapter 2 for more information on using color in
GoLive.*

Hybrid Buttons

Some buttons—those that show a downward-
pointing arrow next to them—are a hybrid
type that either launch commands or open a
menu from which individual options can be
chosen.

Select Window Button

Clicking on the Select Window button, for example, opens the last-opened window. Clicking on its arrow, however, presents a menu-style option list in which any current window may be opened by clicking on the appropriate entry.

Show in Browser Button

Clicking on the Show in Browser button will launch the current Web page in all available Web browsers. However, clicking on its arrow presents a menu-style option list where you can pick a specific Web browser from the list.

Toolbar Changes

The toolbar changes from time to time to reflect the current situation. This, for example, is the toolbar for working with Cascading Style Sheets (CSS).

See Chapter 10 for more information on Cascading Style Sheets.

Using Palettes

The most commonly used palette is the Objects palette.

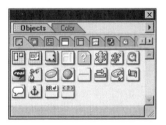

Accessing Palettes

Palettes can be opened by choosing Window from the menu and then clicking on the name of the palette. Currently active palettes are indicated by a checkmark.

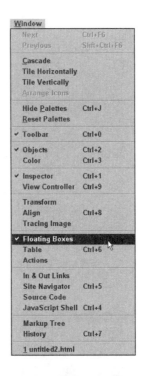

Using the Objects Palette

Clicking on different tabs within the Objects palette gives you access to various specialized icons—in this case, clicking on the Forms tab lets you get to the different items that are used to create forms.

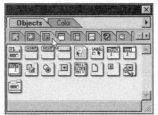

Using the Color Palette

The Color palette can be accessed by clicking on its tab, the color box in the toolbar, or the color boxes in various Inspectors.

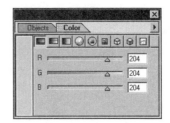

See Chapter 2 for details on using the Color palette.

Grouping Palettes

Several palettes are grouped together, each accessed by clicking on its tab.

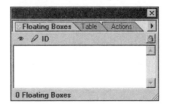

Selecting Palette Tabs

The size of the palette group may change, depending upon which tab is selected.

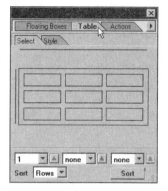

Working with Inspectors

When GoLive is opened, the default Text Inspector is activated. The Inspector tab never says anything except "Inspector"—the particular version is signified by the name in the lower left corner.

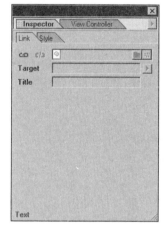

Inspector Contents

Whenever a new object is inserted or selected, the contents of the Inspector change to present the options appropriate for that object.

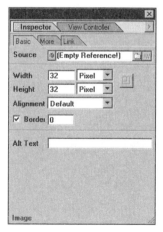

Inspector with Multiple Tabs

When the Inspector contains multiple tabs, click on the tabs to access more options.

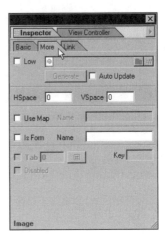

Understanding the Document Window

The Document Window is the canvas on which you create your Web pages. Its different tabs each present a unique way to view or work with your material.

The Document Views

The Document Window's default view is the Layout Editor.

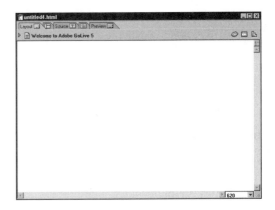

Layout Editor

The Layout Editor is where you type your text and where objects are dragged and dropped from the Objects palette.

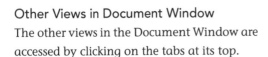

Other Views in Document Window

The other views in the Document Window are accessed by clicking on the tabs at its top.

Frame Editor

The Frame Editor is used for creating framed Web sites.

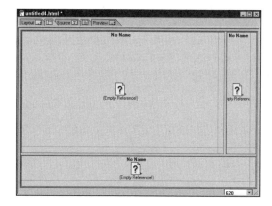

HTML Source Editor

The HTML Source Editor shows the source code which GoLive generates as a result of your actions in the Layout Editor. The source code can be manually altered in this view.

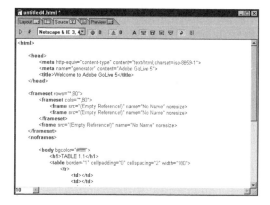

HTML Outline Editor

The HTML Outline Editor shows an outline view of the tags currently found on the Web page. Clicking on the tags' arrows expands and contracts the outline.

Layout Preview

The Layout Preview shows how the page in the Layout Editor will look in a Web browser.

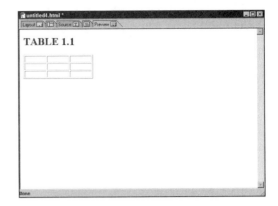

Rearranging the GoLive Interface

Just in case you don't like something about the way GoLive is laid out, it's nice to know that you can change things around and set them up the way you want them.

Floating Elements

All elements in the GoLive interface can be positioned however you want them to be.

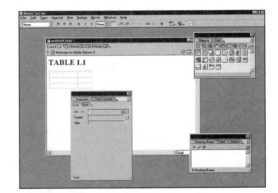

Moving Elements

To move any element—the Document Window, palettes, or the Inspector—click on its title bar and, while holding the mouse button down, drag it into its new position.

Turning the Toolbar into a Floating Element

Even the toolbar can be turned into a floating element. Just click on the drag bars at its left side and, while holding the mouse button down, drag it out.

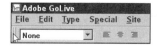

Returning the Toolbar

To return the toolbar to its normal location, double-click on its title bar.

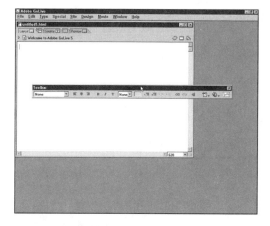

Separating Palettes

Each palette in a group can be pulled out so that it becomes a separate entity. To begin the process, click on the palette's tab.

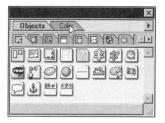

1.

While holding the mouse button down, drag the tab out of the palette grouping. An outline of the palette will follow along.

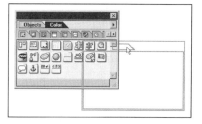

2.

Drop the palette when it is clear of its original group. To return it to the group—or add it to a new group—drag its tab into the group.

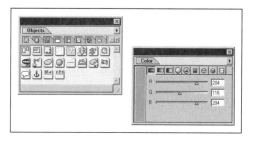

Docking Elements

Unfortunately, having all these palettes around can get in the way of your work. Rather than having to close all the palettes except the one you're currently using, you can simply dock them to keep them out of the way.

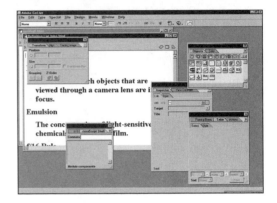

1.

To dock a palette group, Ctrl+click on its title bar.

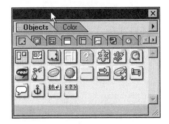

2.

The group's tabs appear sideways at the right-hand side of the screen. To restore the group to its original position, simply click on one of the docked tabs.

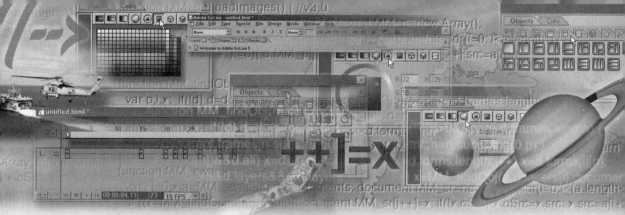

Chapter 2
Creating Pages and Sites

- Create, rename, and save Web pages

- Change the color of elements on a page or within a site

- Set default Web browsers for previewing Web pages

- Create, manage, and maintain Web sites

Working with Web Pages

Individual pages are the heart of any Web site. Regardless of how many different types of files need to be pulled together to make a site, the Web page is still the main method for accessing them.

Opening, Saving, and Creating Pages

The default GoLive Web page is a simple, pretitled blank white page. Its source code also includes information on the default character set and a statement that it was made with GoLive.

```html
<html>

    <head>
        <meta http-equiv="content-type"
        content="text/html;charset=iso-8859-1">
        <meta name="generator"
        content="Adobe GoLive 5">
        <title>Welcome to Adobe GoLive 5</title>
    </head>

    <body bgcolor="#ffffff">
        <p></p>
    </body>

</html>
```

1.

When GoLive first starts up, the default page appears. It has a file name of "untitled.html," even though it has a title of "Welcome to Adobe GoLive 5."

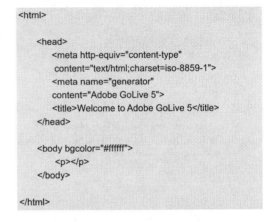

2.

To change the title of the Web page, click on the Page icon at the top left of the Layout Editor.

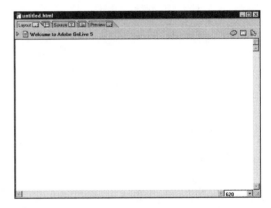

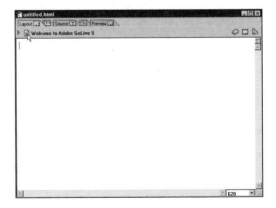

3.

In the Page Inspector, highlight the default title and type your own page title over it.

4.

To change the file name, choose File|Save As from the menu.

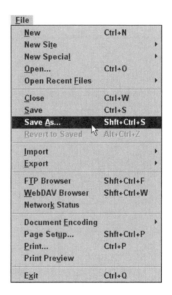

5.

In the Save As dialog box, the "untitled" portion is automatically highlighted. Simply type the new name over it.

6.

GoLive doesn't have the New Page icon so common to other programs, so you have to use the menu (or the keyboard shortcut shown on the menu) to create a new Web page.

7.

If one page already exists, the new page appears over it, but slightly down and to the right.

Working with Color

Color options in GoLive are handled in the Color palette. Each of its nine buttons handles a different aspect of color for items on pages or throughout Web sites.

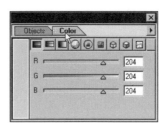

The vertical color bar on the left can be dragged onto colorable objects to set them to that color.

RGB Sliders Button

The first button is the RGB Sliders button. It presents three pairs of sliders and text boxes. The amount of red, green, or blue in a color can be set either by dragging the sliders or by entering the amount in the text boxes.

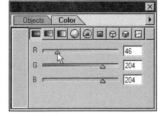

CMYK Sliders Button

The CMYK Sliders button works the same way as the RGB Sliders button, except that the color is set by the amounts of cyan, magenta, yellow, and black in it.

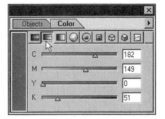

Gray Slider Button

The Gray Slider button also works by using either a slider or the direct entry of the value in the text box, but it is limited to setting the amount of white in a grayscale.

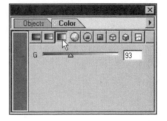

HSB Wheel Button

The HSB Wheel button lets you pick a color by clicking on a color wheel. The brightness of that color is then set by either using the slider or typing a value into the Brightness text box.

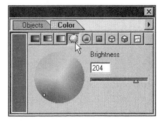

HSV Picker Button

With the HSV Picker button, you click on the circle to choose a color, and then you click within the square to set the saturation (less to the left, more to the right) and value (darker to the bottom). Values may also be entered directly into the text boxes.

Palettes Button

The Palettes button presents a simple chart from which colors may be chosen by clicking on the squares. Click on the arrow button to the right of the chart to choose which color set to use.

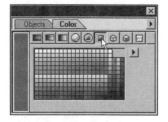

Web Color List Button

The Web Color List button presents the standard 216 "Web safe" colors, which theoretically display the same at any color resolution from 256 colors on up. Click on the color chart, scroll the listing, and click on a color bar; or you can enter the value in the text box.

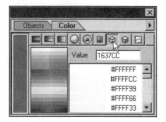

Web Name List Button

The Web Name List button presents a list of named colors. Scroll down and click on a color bar. Alternatively, enter the color name in the Name text box or its hexadecimal number in the Value text box.

Site Colors Button

The Site Colors button is blank if no site is open. If a site is open and you have added colors to the Site Window's color tab, they appear here.

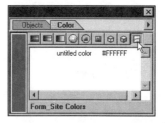

Previewing and Browser Testing

The quickest way to check the appearance of your Web pages in GoLive is to click on the Preview tab, but you should also check them in the Web browsers you expect your audience to use.

1.

Before you can use GoLive to check a page in a Web browser, you need to set your browser preferences. Select Edit|Preferences from the menu to get started.

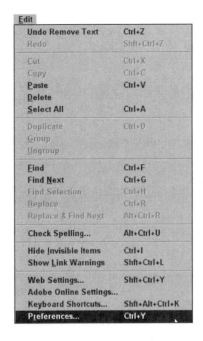

2.

In the Preferences dialog box, click on Browsers. At first, none will be listed in the right-hand pane, so you need to click on the Find All button below that pane.

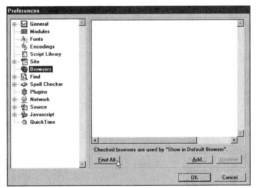

3.

GoLive will search your system for Web browsers and add any it finds to the listing. To specify one or more of them as default browsers for testing, click in the checkbox to the left of the browser name.

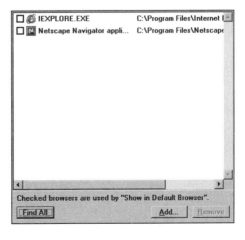

4.

Click on the OK button to confirm your choices.

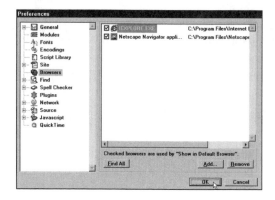

5.

Click on the Show In Browser button in the toolbar to launch the default testing browsers. If multiple browsers are available, you can launch just one of them by clicking on the arrow next to the button and selecting the browser from the pop-up menu.

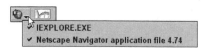

Managing Web Sites

A Web site—the amalgamation of several Web pages—is the ultimate goal of most Web page creation. GoLive is designed not only to create individual pages, but also to manage Web sites.

Creating a Site

The Site Window is where GoLive brings together all the information regarding the files found in a Web site. It opens automatically whenever a site is created or opened.

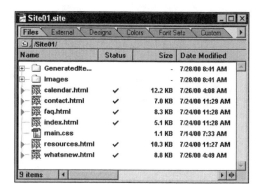

Site Options

To create a site, choose File|New Site from the menu. From the submenu, choose Blank, Import from Folder, Copy from Template, or Import from FTP Server.

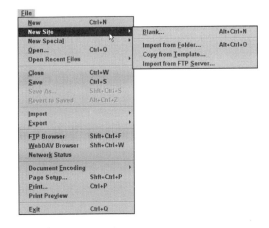

Blank Options

If you selected the Blank option, you will be asked to name the site and to choose a folder that will hold the site's files.

Import from Folder Option

If you chose the Import from Folder option, you will need to specify the folder to be used and which file in that folder is the home page.

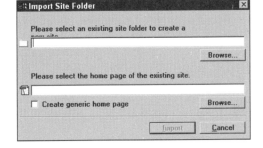

Copy from Template Option

If you picked the Copy from Template option, you will be presented with a list of existing site templates from which to choose.

You must name the site in this dialog box.

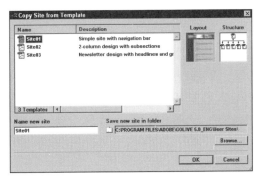

Import from FTP Server Option

If you chose the Import from FTP Server option, you will be asked to provide the information necessary to connect with that server. Once connected, you will have to specify which file is the home page.

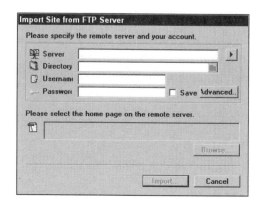

Using the Site Window

The basic Site Window can be altered to include more detailed information by clicking on the double arrow in the lower right corner; it fails to expand in size, so you need to manually resize it to make it useful.

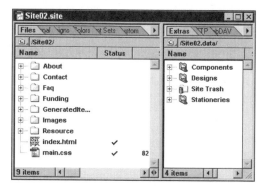

Site Window Tabs

The basic Site Window has six tabs—Files, External, Designs, Colors, Font Sets, and Custom.

If you're exploring sites for the first time, you should open one of the sample sites using the Copy from Template option described in the preceding section. That will make it easier to see all the Site Window's functions.

Files Tab

The Files tab lists the files and subfolders that are found within the Web site. Individual folders can be expanded and contracted by clicking on the plus and minus signs.

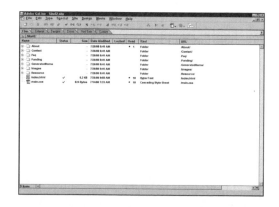

External Tab

The External tab holds the URLs for regular links and mailto links. It can be populated manually or by selecting a page within the site and pressing the F5 key.

You can import a favorites or bookmarks file by using File|Import|Favorites as Site Externals.

URLs and External Tab

To manually add URLs, click on the Site tab of the Objects palette, and then drag the URL icon from there into the External tab of the Site Window.

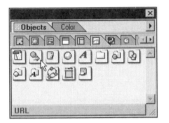

Design Tab

The Design tab shows all currently existing designs for this site.

To make a new design, choose Design|New Site Design from the menu.

Elements and Design Tab

Double-click on the design name to open the Design Window, and then drag elements from the Site tab of the Objects palette into the Design Window.

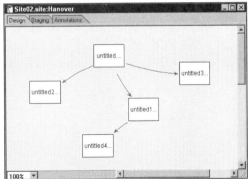

Color Tab

The Site Window's Colors tab shows all the colors used in the site. Drag colors from the Color palette or drag colored elements and drop them here to add to the list.

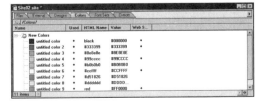

Fonts Sets Tab

The Font Sets tab shows the different font sets that are used in the site. To add a new font set, drag some text that uses the font set from your Web page into this tab.

Custom Tab

The Custom tab holds Web page segments, called "snippets," that you can reuse on other pages. To add a snippet, drag the section you want to reuse (or its source code) into the Custom tab.

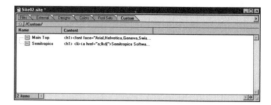

Using Navigation View

The Navigation View provides you with an overall view of the parent-child relationships among the pages in your Web site.

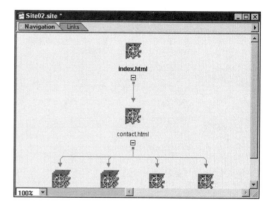

1.

To get into Navigation View, open a site, and then click on the Navigation View button in the toolbar.

2.

At first, the only thing showing in the Navigation View is the site's home page icon.

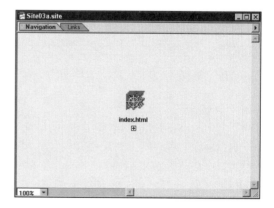

3.

Click on the plus sign underneath the home page icon to expand the view's coverage of the other pages in the site. Do the same with the plus signs under other icons to fully expand the coverage.

To expand all at once, click on any page, and then click on the Unfold All button in the toolbar.

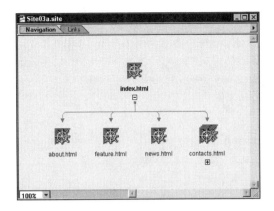

4.

To reposition a page in the navigational hierarchy, drag it from its current position onto another page and drop it there.

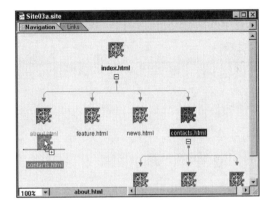

5.

All subordinate pages in the navigational hierarchy are moved along with the parent page.

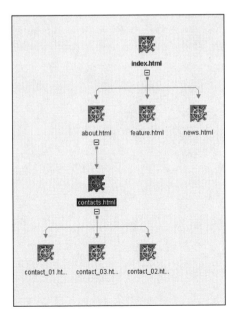

6.

Click on the New Previous Page button to add another Web page that is on the same level of the navigational hierarchy, but before the current one.

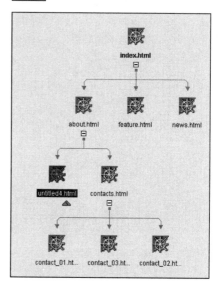

7.

Click on the New Next Page button to add another Web page that is on the same level of the navigational hierarchy, but after the current one.

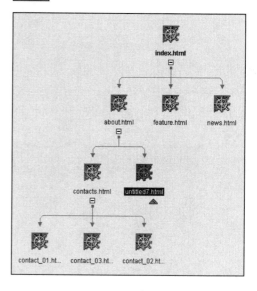

8.

Click on the New Parent Page button to add another Web page that is on the next highest level of the navigational hierarchy.

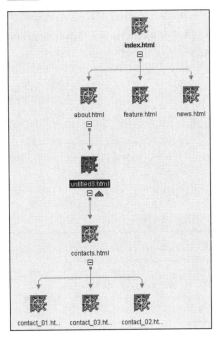

9.

Click on the New Child Page button to add another Web page that is on the next lowest level of the navigational hierarchy.

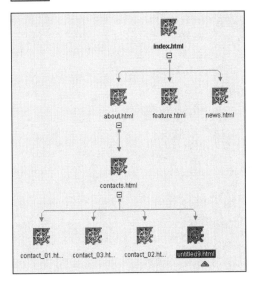

Using Links View

Links View shows the links that go to and from the pages in the site. Even a partially expanded view of all the links in a single Web site can be an incredibly complex display.

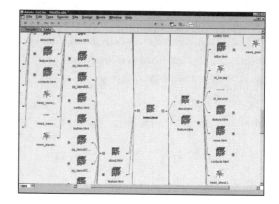

1.

To change from Navigation View to Links View, click on the Links tab.

Or choose Site|View|Links from the menu.

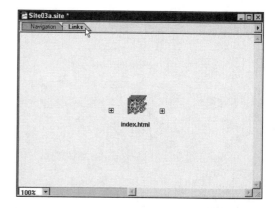

2.

Click on the right-hand plus sign next to the home page icon to show all links from the home page to other files, including embedded files (such as icons).

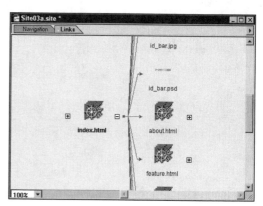

3.

Click on the left-hand plus sign next to the home page icon to show all files with links coming into the home page.

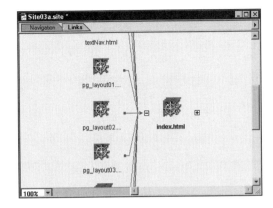

4.

Continue to click on the plus signs next to each page to expand the Links View. Click on the minus signs that replace them to shrink the view again.

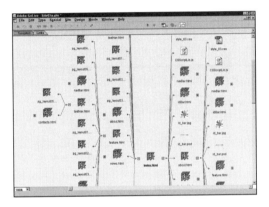

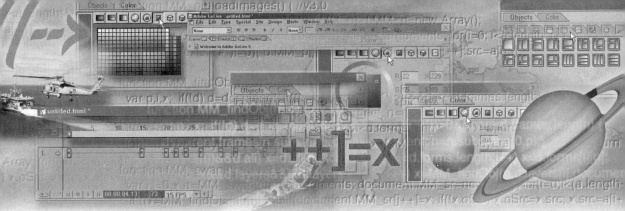

Chapter 3
Working with Text

- Entering text in the Layout view by typing, pasting, and dragging and dropping

- Formatting text with block level and text level elements

- Changing text alignment, size, and color

- Picking font sets

- Spellchecking and searching and replacing

Words on the Web

Words are the most important part of a Web page. Without them, the World Wide Web would be nothing but an electronic picture gallery. Even if you have a highly graphical site, you need to know how to work with text in GoLive.

Getting Text on the Page

You can type your text in by hand, paste copied material into place, or use drag and drop to transfer text from one application to another.

Entering Text

The most common way to add text to a Web page is simply to type it in.

Activating Text Cursor

When GoLive starts up, the text cursor is active and you can immediately type. If, however, you type values into any of the palettes during the course of your work, you'll need to click in the Layout area to reactivate your text cursor.

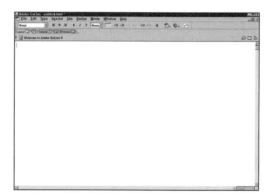

Placing Text Cursor

If the page is blank, the text cursor will remain in the upper left corner no matter where you click on the page. If the page has material on it, the cursor will land wherever you click. (If you click below the last element, the cursor will go to the end of that element.)

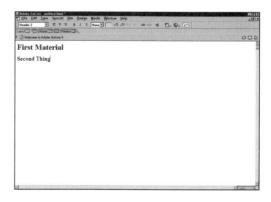

Using the Insertion Point

The location of the text cursor is the *insertion point*. Anything you type or paste will show up where you have placed the cursor.

You can use this fact to quickly edit a word by clicking in the middle of it first.

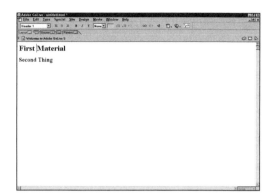

Dragging and Dropping Text

Text in GoLive can be dragged from one location and dropped into another. Also, text from any other application that supports drag and drop can be moved between open application windows.

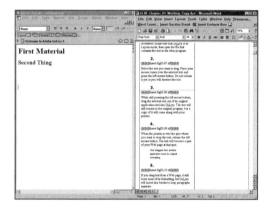

1.

To drag text from another application into GoLive, start both programs and arrange the two windows so that both programs are accessible. Make sure GoLive is in Layout mode, and then open the file that contains the text in the other program.

2.

Select the text you want to drag. Place your mouse cursor over the selected text and press the left mouse button. Do not release it yet or you will deselect the text.

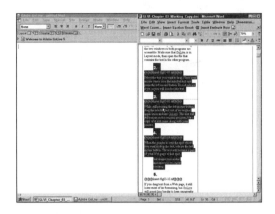

3.

While still pressing the left mouse button, drag the selected text out of its original application and into GoLive. The text will still remain in the original program, but a copy of it will come along with your pointer.

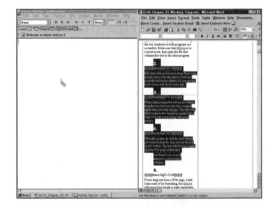

4.

When the pointer is over the spot where you want to drop the text, release the left mouse button. The text will become a part of your Web page at that spot.

Text dragged from another application loses its original formatting in GoLive.

5.

To move text within GoLive, drag selected text from one part of the Layout area to another. This is not quite like dragging text from a second program. In this case, the text is actually removed from its original location.

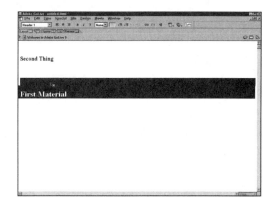

Formatting Text

You can use two different kinds of elements to format text—block level elements and text level elements.

Formatting with Block Level Elements

Block level elements affect the structure of a Web page. They each start on a new line and cannot be contained within other block level elements.

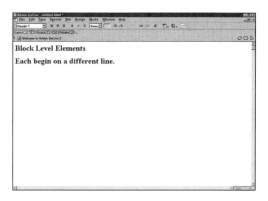

Block Level Elements in the Drop-down List

There are nine block level elements in the Paragraph Format drop-down list.

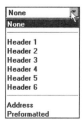

Block Level Elements in the Menu

The same block level elements are accessible via the Type|Header menu option.

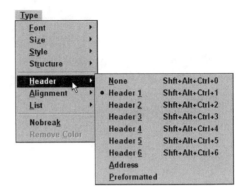

Header Elements

The Header elements (H1 through H6 in HTML parlance) set up various sizes of text in bold style. Headers 3 through 6 are rarely used because they don't offer a distinct difference from normal text.

Headers 3 through 6, however, are used quite often when you design for those with sight disabilities. A reader program distinguishes the tone of a header but doesn't with normal text.

Header 1

Normal text.

Header 2

Normal text.

Header 3

Normal text.

Header 4

Normal text.

Header 5

Normal text.

Header 6

Normal text.

"None" Style

The source code shows that the "None" style is actually a P (paragraph) element, the usual way of showing text on a Web page.

```
<h1>Header 1</h1>
<p>Normal text.</p>
<h2>Header 2</h2>
<p>Normal text.</p>
<h3>Header 3</h3>
<p>Normal text.</p>
<h4>Header 4</h4>
<p>Normal text.</p>
<h5>Header 5</h5>
<p>Normal text.</p>
<h6>Header 6</h6>
<p>Normal text.</p>
<p></p>
```

ADDRESS Element

The ADDRESS element looks like plain italics, but a trifle larger.

This is in Address format.

This is just plain Italics.

Although you can achieve nearly the same look with italics, the content of an ADDRESS element will be catalogued differently by sophisticated programs.

Preformatted Text

Preformatted text is represented by the PRE element in the HTML source code. It is used to present the text in a fixed width font instead of the variable width font that is normally used for text on Web pages. Preformatted text is longer than normal text because of the spacing.

`This is in Preformatted format.`

This is not in Preformatted format.

Formatting with Horizontal Lines

The horizontal line is another block level element that is commonly used on Web pages. Although it's not strictly a textual element, it is often used to emphasize headings or to separate paragraphs.

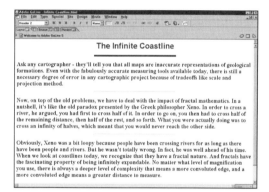

1.

You insert a horizontal line by dragging the Line icon from the Basics tab of the Objects palette and dropping it onto your Web page. You can also place your text cursor where you want the line to appear and then double-click on the Line icon.

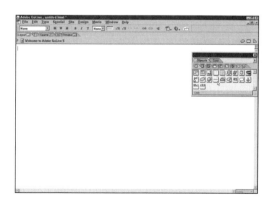

2.

If the Inspector isn't showing, choose Window|Inspector from the menu.

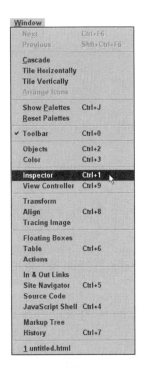

3.

The default line type is 3D, or hollow. Click on the left Style button if you prefer a solid line. Click on the right Style button to restore the line to hollow style.

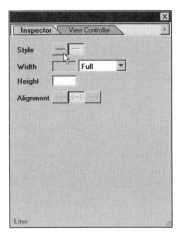

4.

If you do not want the line to extend across the entire Web page, click on the drop-down Width list. Select Percent to set a width that is a percentage of the Web page's width. Select Pixel to set the line to an absolute width.

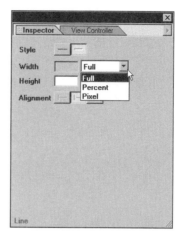

5.

The Width text box is now activated. Click within it and enter the percentage or pixel values for the line width.

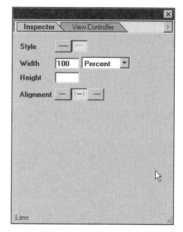

6.

To set a specific line height, click within the Height text box and type in a value. This must be the number of pixels; there is no percentage option for line height.

Different browsers have different default values for line height, so it's a good idea to specify a value.

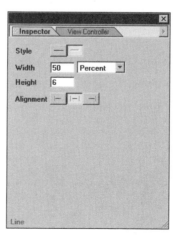

7.

By default, lines are centered. To change the alignment, click on one of the alignment buttons in the Inspector.

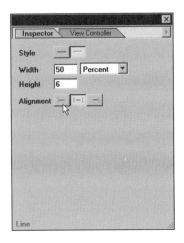

Formatting with Text Level Elements

| Text *level* elements **don't start new lines.** |

Text level elements, also known as *inline elements,* don't start new lines, but are contained within block level elements.

Text Level Elements

Nine text level elements are available in the Type|Style menu option. The Bold, Italic, and Teletype options are also available from the toolbar (the B, I, and T buttons).

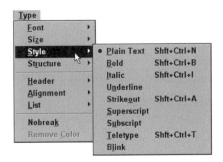

Internet Explorer and Text Level Elements

Different Web browsers render the effects differently. Here's how Internet Explorer shows them.

The Blink style flashes text on and off in Netscape Navigator only. It has no effect in Internet Explorer.

Netscape Navigator and Text Level Elements

Here's how Netscape Navigator shows the same text styles.

Most people find blinking text annoying.

Type|Structure Menu Options

There are nine more text level elements in the Type|Structure menu option.

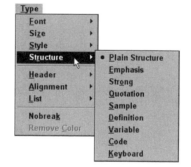

Type|Structure Options in Internet Explorer

As you can see, many of the Type|Structure choices produce similar or identical effects to the Type|Style choices when rendered in Internet Explorer.

Type|Structure Options in Netscape Navigator

The same is true of these text styles when they are rendered in Netscape Navigator.

Plain Structure

Emphasis

Strong

Quotation

Sample

Definition

Variable

Code

Keyboard

Removing Formatting from Text

If you have assigned bold, italic, or teletype styles to text, you can remove the formatting by selecting the text and clicking on the B, I, or T buttons in the toolbar.

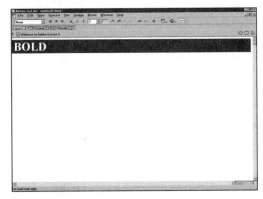

1.

To remove any Style formatting, select the text, choose Type|Style from the menu, and click on Plain Text.

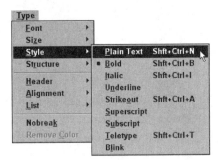

2.

To remove any Structure formatting, select the text, choose Type|Structure from the menu, and click on Plain Structure.

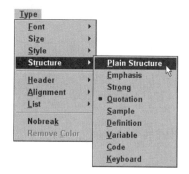

3.

To remove any Header formatting, select the text, choose Type|Header from the menu, and click on None.

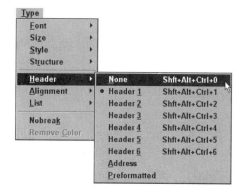

Formatting with Nobreak

Text on a Web page normally breaks—that is, wraps around to the next line—at whatever space happens to be nearest to the right margin. If you have terms you don't want to be separated, use the Nobreak option to force them to stay together.

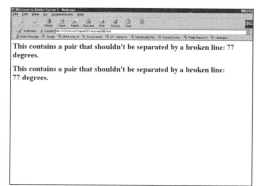

1.

Select the text you want to keep together.

It's a good idea to keep nonbreaking sections small. Nobreak will force users to scroll horizontally to read the text if it's applied to a very large section.

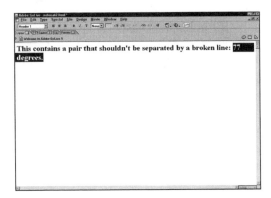

2.

Choose Type|Nobreak from the menu.

Apply nobreak only after all the text is written. You can't add any text to the very beginning of a nobreak section if it's at the beginning of a paragraph.

3.

The nonbreaking section will be kept together.

Make sure to test the page in your target browsers to see if it looks right. The representation in GoLive is not necessarily the same as you'll get in a browser.

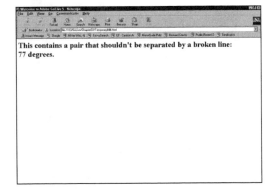

Formatting with Line Breaks

A small amount of extra vertical space is normally inserted between two paragraphs on a Web page. Line breaks allow you to add more.

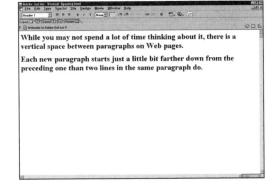

1.

To add a line break, place your text cursor where you want the break to appear, and then double-click on the Line Break icon in the Basics tab of the Objects palette, or you can drag the icon to the desired insertion point.

You can also use the Shift+Enter key combination to insert a line break.

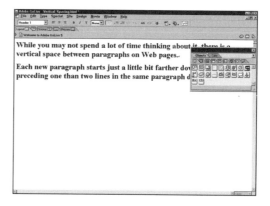

2.

GoLive's line break symbol will appear and any text following it will automatically move down past the blank line the symbol represents.

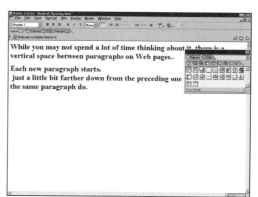

3.

A line break also can be inserted into a line of text to force all the text following it to move down one line—which was its originally intended use, actually. If the line break is inserted before a blank space, the next line will start with a space, but that space won't show in a Web browser.

Changing Text

You can just slap text onto your Web page and leave it in the plain vanilla style, or you can change the alignment, size, and color to suit yourself.

Aligning Text

By default, all text is left aligned, meaning that it starts at the left margin. You can also center it or right align it.

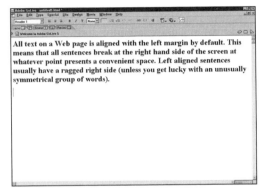

1.

The ends of center-aligned sentences are equally spaced from both margins. In the case of a paragraph, this can produce a ragged appearance.

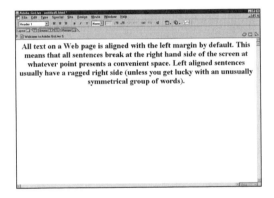

2.

Here's right-aligned text. Note that the sentences are neither longer nor shorter than with the default settings, but end on the right margin just as they would normally begin on the left margin.

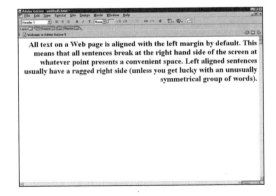

3.

Selecting a left alignment results in the same appearance as when no alignment is chosen, but the HTML source code shows a difference in specifically setting the alignment to "Left."

```
<div align="left">
<h1>All text on a Web page is aligned with the
left margin by default. This means that all
sentences break at the right hand side of the
screen at whatever point presents a
convenient space. Left aligned sentences
usually have a ragged right side (unless you
get lucky with an unusually symmetrical group
of words).</h1>
</div>
```

Indenting Text

No matter how many times you hit your Tab key in GoLive, it won't indent your text one inch. To do so, you have to use Block Indent.

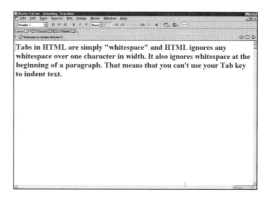

1.

Place the text cursor in the paragraph you want to indent, and then select Type| Alignment|Increase Block Indent from the menu.

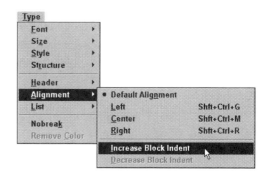

2.

Both sides of the paragraph are indented from their respective margins. Although this seems similar to centering, the sentences maintain normal edges when indented.

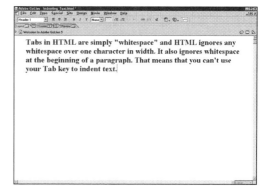

3.

To indent more, repeat Step 1. To unindent, select Type|Alignment|Decrease Block Indent from the menu. To remove all indentation, you need to decrease once for each time you increased.

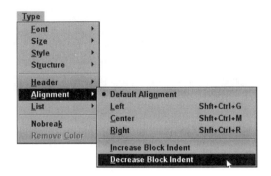

Changing Font Size and Color

You're not limited to the default font sizes. When it suits you, you can enlarge or shrink anything from a single character to a whole page of text, and you can make any of it any color you want.

Changing Font Size

To resize text, select the text you wish to change, and then click on the Font Size drop-down list. To set a constant size, click on one of the numbers (1 through 7) in the top segment of the list.

1.

To set a size that is relative to the base size of normal characters, click on one of the numbers with a plus or minus sign. The base character size is 3, so if you choose -1, you're setting the selected text to size 2.

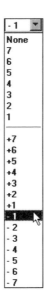

2.

No character can be larger than size 7 or less than size 1, regardless of relative values. For example, if you add a +6 to a character and the base character size is 3, you don't get a size 9—just a size 7.

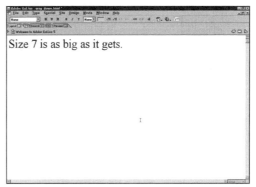

Changing Color

To set color, select the text you want to work with, and then click on the Text Color button in the toolbar. See Chapter 2 for details on how to choose colors.

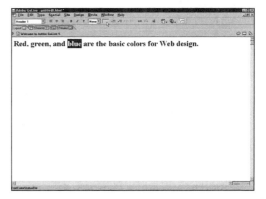

Removing Color

To remove color, select the colored text and choose Type|Remove Color from the menu.

Working with Font Sets

Three basic font types are used on Web pages, but different computers and operating systems don't agree on what they are. Here's how to make sure that people see what you intended for them to see, regardless of whether they're using a PC, a Mac, or a Unix or Linux box.

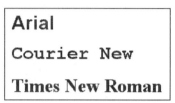

1.

Select the text you want to specify a font for, and then choose Type|Font from the menu. Click on the desired font face in the submenu to change the selected text to that font.

2.

The appearance of the font is altered on the Web page.

Default Font
Reset to Arial

3.

Several font options are actually included in the source code when you set a font. This allows the user's Web browser to display a similar font if your first choice is unavailable.

```
<font face="Arial,Helvetica,Geneva,Swiss,
SunSans-Regular">Reset to Arial</font>
```

Changing Words

After you've done all the fancy things you can do with your textual characters, headings, paragraphs, and the like, it's time to pay attention to the words themselves.

Checking Spelling

It's a fakt. The wey we spel things makes an impreshun on pepul. To make sure you make the right impression, use the spellchecker.

> **Eckspurt Ottomotive Suply**
>
> **Our Moto: Trust Us Wit Yur Kar**

1.

Choose Edit|Check Spelling from the menu. This brings up the Check Spelling dialog box.

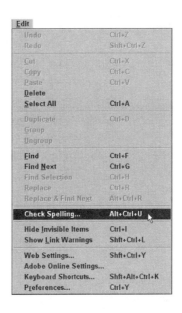

2.

Click on the Start button.

If you want spellchecking to begin from the current position of the text cursor, deselect the From Top checkbox. You can also access more options by clicking on the blue arrowhead in the lower left corner.

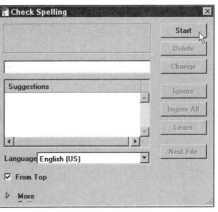

3.

When the spellchecker finds a word that isn't in its dictionary, it suggests a replacement and lists other alternatives. Click on Change to accept the replacement. Click on Delete to erase the word.

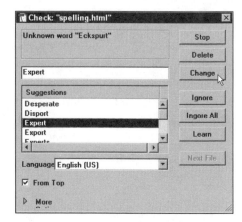

4.

If the word is spelled correctly, click on Learn to add the word to the dictionary. Click on Ignore to move on without adding it (or Ignore All to avoid having to do it over again every time the word appears).

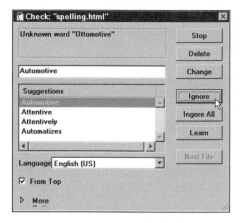

Searching and Replacing

When you need to make changes, it's nice to know that GoLive is designed to help you make them easily. You can do a quick search by selecting a word or phrase and choosing Edit|Find Selection from the menu.

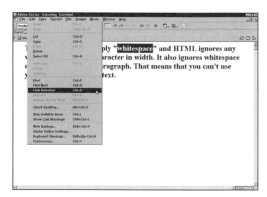

1.

For more powerful searching options, choose Edit|Find from the menu.

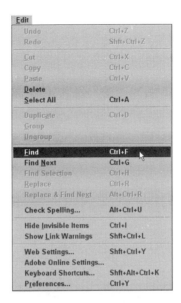

2.

Check any options you want active, and then enter the search term in the text area. If you're just searching, click the Find button.

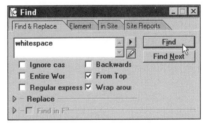

3.

If you want to search and replace, click on the blue arrowhead next to the word Replace to expand the dialog box. Enter the replacement term in the newly revealed text area.

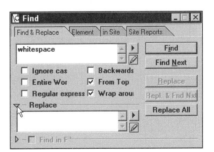

4.

To search, click on the Find button. When a term is found, GoLive highlights it and stops the search. If you want to look for another occurrence of the search term, click on Find Next.

Unless you move the Find dialog box to the side of the Layout Editor, it will go behind the Layout Editor when a term is found. You can retrieve it by clicking on Window|Find in the menu.

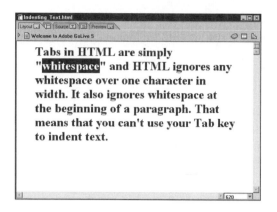

5.

If you are doing a search and replace, click on the Replace button to replace the term. Click on the Repl. & Fnd Nxt button to replace and continue the search. To automatically replace all occurrences of the search term, click on the Replace All button.

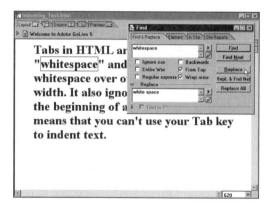

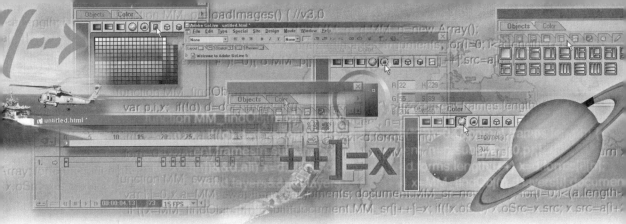

Chapter 4
Making Lists

- Create three types of lists

- Customize a list structure to fit your needs

- Explore the limits of list contents

Understanding List Types

GoLive supports both of the commonly used types of lists as well as a little-used third kind. The most popular type of list is undoubtedly the *numbered list*. Numbered lists are called *ordered lists* in HTML, because they're used to present a sequence of steps that must be followed in a particular order. You'll see them in the source code as OL elements. Within each OL element, the individual list items are contained within LI elements.

An *unnumbered list* is what is usually thought of as a bulleted list, where each list item is denoted by a symbol such as a solid circle. These lists are used when the order of the steps doesn't matter. HTML calls them *unordered lists,* and they're represented by the UL element in the source code. Just as with numbered lists, the contents are composed of LI elements.

Creating Numbered Lists

Numbered lists aren't supposed to be used for things where the ranking or sequence doesn't matter, like "to do" lists or parts lists. They're best used for things like the kinds of step-by-step procedures that are presented in this book.

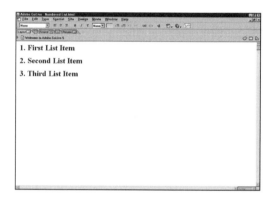

1.

The easiest way to put a numbered list onto your Web page is to use the button approach. To do this, place your text cursor where you want to insert the list, and then click on the Numbered List button in the toolbar.

2.

The number 1 will appear at the insertion point. Type in the text for the first list item. Next, press your Enter key. This creates a second list item labeled with the number 2. As you continue to type new list items and press Enter, the number on the new line will always be the next increment.

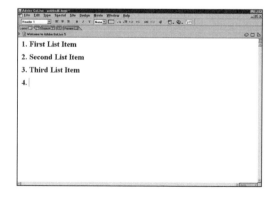

3.

If something else is already on the page below the list, all you have to do to finish is to click on any of the other elements.

If nothing is below the list, press Enter after you complete the final list item. Next, click on the Decrease List Level button in the toolbar. The numbered line will convert to a normal blank one.

Creating Unnumbered Lists

Unnumbered lists are created in the same way as numbered lists, with two obvious exceptions:

- You click on the Unnumbered List button (which is immediately to the right of the Numbered List button).

- Bullets appear instead of numbers.

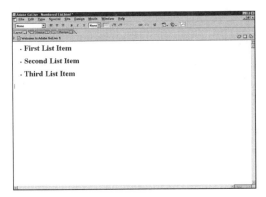

Changing Bullet and Number Systems

By default, numbered lists use Arabic numerals and unnumbered lists use bullets that are solid circles. You do have other options, however, such as using letters for numbered lists.

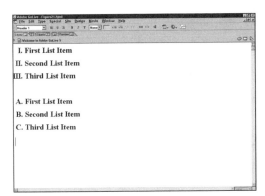

1.

Select the list you want to modify.

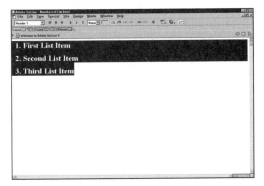

It's hard to imagine a use for this trick, but you can change the bullet or number style for individual list items or a group of list items by selecting them instead of the entire list.

2.

Right-click (Mac users Control+click) on the selected area and choose List from the pop-up menu. The submenu that appears includes every option for formatting lists.

Explore the possibilities by selecting different options.

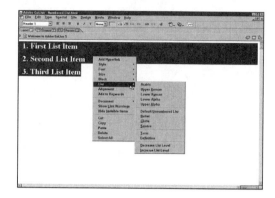

3.

Click on the option you want in the submenu. The list will instantly change to the selected format. These are the main options:

- *Arabic*—1, 2, 3....
- *Upper Roman*—I, II, III....
- *Lower Alpha*—a, b, c....
- *Upper Alpha*—A, B, C....
- *Bullet*—Solid circle
- *Circle*—Hollow circle
- *Square*—Hollow box

The same options are available from the menu bar by selecting Type|List.

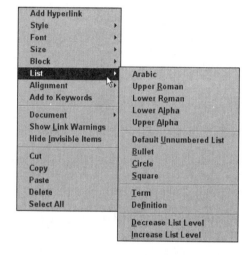

Changing the Level of a List Item

In many cases, you might want to have a list where some or all of the list items have their own subsections. A single step, for example, may be composed of a series of smaller steps. Or perhaps a single step involves handling a number of different ingredients or parts. We'll show you how to create this example.

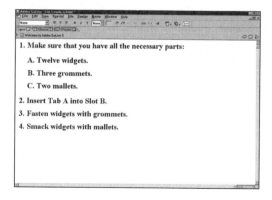

1.

Remember how you used the Decrease List Level button to end lists? You use it and its partner, the Increase List Level button, to indent and unindent list items. First, create the list, then select the items you want to indent. Next, click on the Increase List Level button in the toolbar.

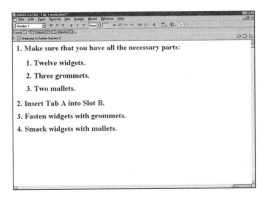

2.

You now have two different lists, one of which is embedded within the other. The numbering on the main list has changed properly to reflect the new arrangement. However, the sublist is also a numbered list, and this creates a potentially confusing situation for anyone attempting to follow the steps.

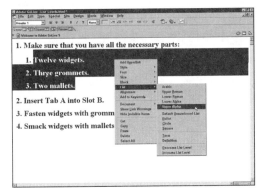

3.

Right-click on the selected area and choose the desired list format from the pop-up menu. For this example, we chose Upper Alpha. Technically, the ordering (A, B, C) isn't necessary for these whimsical instructions; an unnumbered list would do quite well here. The process for creating an embedded bulleted list, however, works a little bit differently.

4.

Select the list items you want to indent, then click on the Increase List Level button. Next, click on the Unnumbered List button.

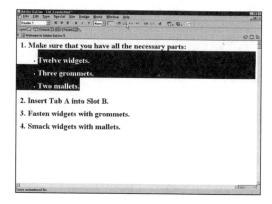

5.

If you start with a bulleted list, each level of indentation changes the bullet. The first level is a solid circle, the second a hollow circle, and from the third on in, a hollow square.

To make an embedded list merge back into the parent list, select the embedded list and click on the Decrease List Level button until the merge is complete and the numbering system falls back into the original scheme.

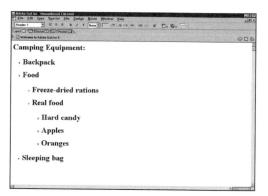

Definition Lists

A *definition list* is used for making glossaries, dictionaries, or any other situation where you need to set up a term and its definition in a distinctive format. Unlike numbered and unnumbered lists, the toolbar has no icon for definition lists. This means that definition lists take a bit more work to create in GoLive than do the other two kinds of lists.

Making Glossaries with Definition Lists

This is one of those things in GoLive that just don't work the way it seems it should. The creation of definition lists could be automated, but instead it's a strictly manual operation. For a short list of terms and definitions, that's not too bad, but if you have a long list, it can become pretty tedious.

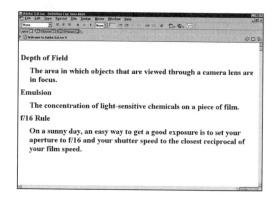

1.

Definition lists consist of terms and their definitions. Definition lists are shown in the source code by the DL element. Within this, terms are denoted by the DT element and definitions by the DD element. The term (DT) must come first, followed by the definition (DD), and then the pattern repeats for each subsequent pair.

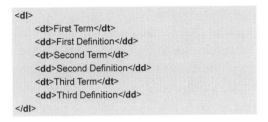

2.

Because GoLive will not automatically alternate between DT and DD elements, you have to assign the appropriate list style to each list item. The easiest approach is to enter all the terms and definitions first, then select the entire list.

Right-click on the selected list and select List|Term from the pop-up menu. You will now have all the list items set up as DT elements.

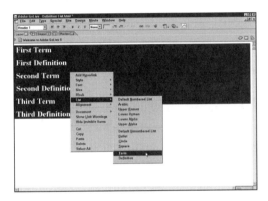

3.

Next, select each definition one at a time. Right-click on it and select List|Definition from the pop-up menu. Because the pop-up menu is dynamic and adjusts to reflect the current situation, the Term option will not show up at all. As each definition is assigned its proper style, it will indent.

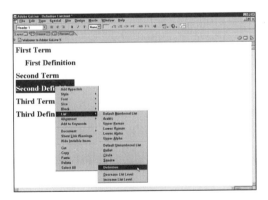

Pushing Lists to the Limit

Everyone thinks of lists as things that simply contain text. The truth is, though, that lists can contain just about anything you can throw at them.

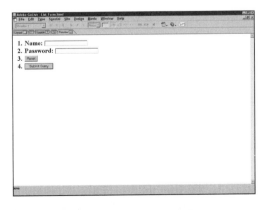

Links in a List

You might want to try putting links into a list. This works best using numbered lists with a ranking system like a top-ranked list. Although you can also put links into an unnumbered list, your visitors may think the bullets are icons that they can click on to activate the links.

Images in a List

There aren't many practical uses for putting images into a list format, but just in case you have a better idea, we thought we should mention it. Any image used in a list should be very short, because too much vertical distance between list items disrupts the flow of the list. This example uses company logos as image links.

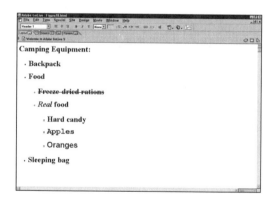

Formatting in a List

Even if all you do with lists is to put text into them, you can still dress them up by formatting the list items. Italicize them, make them bold, change the fonts, or lay some color on. And if you apply a list style to existing text, the text keeps its original styles as well as becoming part of a list.

You can format an entire list, too. Every figure in this chapter uses lists formatted with Header 1 style to improve readability.

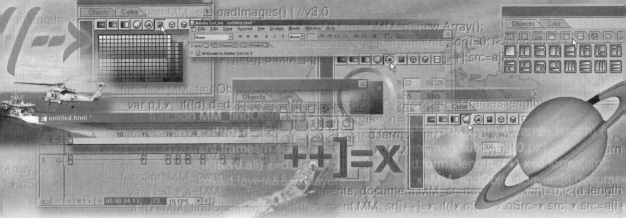

Chapter 5
Adding Images

- Learn how to insert images onto your Web pages

- Dig into the intricacies of image alignment

- Resize images and change their spacing on the page

Adding Images

The three image file formats commonly used on the World Wide Web are GIF, JPEG (also called JPG), and PNG. Although GoLive allows you to import other formats, they won't display in most Web browsers, so it's best to use one of the correct formats to begin with.

Inserting Images

Images are a critical part of most Web pages. Whether they're photographs or line art, they add a powerful visual dimension that plain text can't supply.

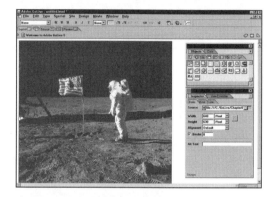

1.

To add an image, place your text cursor where you want to insert the image, and then double-click on the Image icon in the Basic tab of the Objects palette. You can also drag the Image icon onto the page.

2.

The empty image placeholder will appear on the page at the insertion point.

3.

If the Image Inspector is not showing, bring it up by choosing Window|Inspector from the menu.

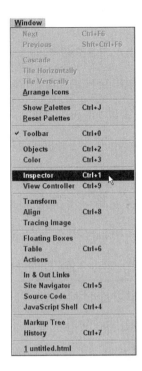

4.

Click on the Browse icon in the Image Inspector.

Note that the image width and height are set to 32 pixels each. This is merely a default setting and will automatically change when an image file is selected.

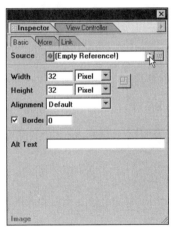

5.

Navigate to the folder for the image file, and then select the file and click on the Open button. Alternatively, simply double-click on the file name.

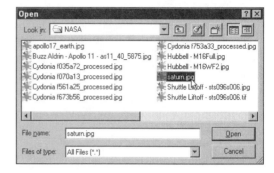

6.

The selected image now displays on the Web page in GoLive.

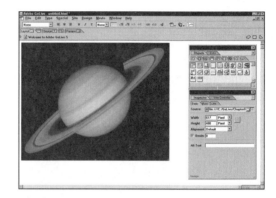

7.

The file location, as well as the actual width and height measurements for the inserted image, are now reflected in the Image Inspector.

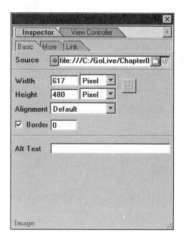

You can replace an existing image by selecting it and then inserting another image over it.

Using Alternative Methods

Two alternative methods for inserting files are the point and shoot and the drag and drop. The point and shoot method described in the steps that follow can be used to insert images only from the Site Window; drag and drop, described later, is more flexible.

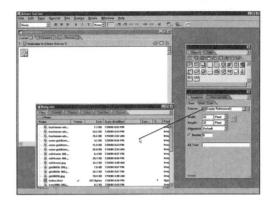

Using Point and Shoot

After an image icon has been placed on the Web page and the Site Window is open, the point and shoot button in the Image Inspector can be used.

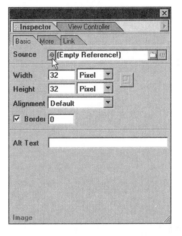

Choose Window|Site Navigator from the menu to open the Site Window. Alternatively, use Ctrl+F5 (Command+F5 for Mac users).

1.

The Layout area and the Site Window must be resized so that they are both accessible at the same time.

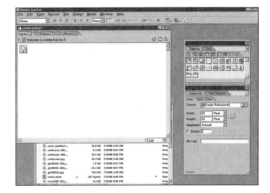

2.

Click on the point and shoot button and keep holding the mouse button down. Drag the pointing line to the image file name in the Site Window.

If the Site Window is partially obscured by the Layout area (as in the preceding figure), it will come to the top.

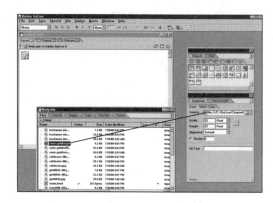

3.

Release the mouse button. The selected image will appear on the Web page, and the Layout area will come to the top.

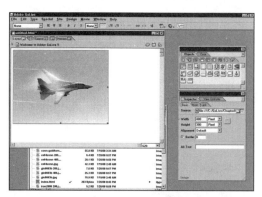

Using the Drag and Drop Method

To use drag and drop, click on the desired image file name in the Site Window. While still holding down the mouse button, drag the file name into the Layout area, and then release the mouse button to drop the image onto the page.

You can also use drag and drop from the file listings in Windows Explorer.

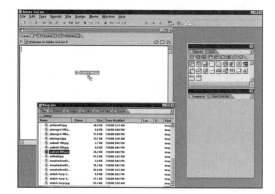

Aligning Images

Image alignment is one of those tricky things that can throw off even the most experienced Web designers. Although images are often treated as if they were block level elements, they are actually inline elements, and most of the image alignment options affect how text fits around images.

Using Image Alignment Options

Although it's possible to do it, you'll rarely see an image tossed into the middle of a paragraph of text, because its size disrupts the flow by pushing down the sentence that contains it.

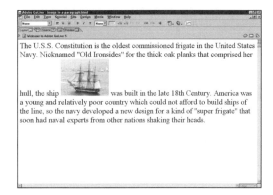

1.

To set the alignment of an image, first select it and then click on the Alignment drop-down list in the Image Inspector.

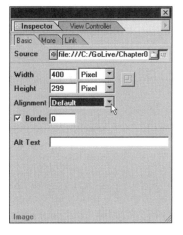

2.

Choose one of the alignments from the list by clicking on it.

Default alignment is the same as Bottom alignment. Technically, under the HTML standard, a Web browser could use a different default, but none do.

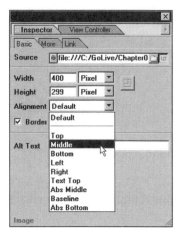

Top Alignment

Top alignment puts the top of the highest letters in the text on the same level as the top of the image.

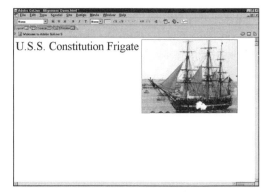

Middle Alignment

Middle alignment puts the baseline of the text on an imaginary line through the middle of the image.

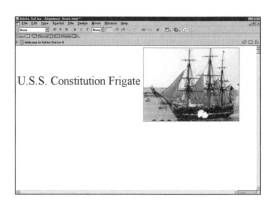

Bottom Alignment

Bottom alignment puts the baseline of the text on the same level as the bottom of the image. The bottoms of letters such as the "g" in the word "Frigate" drop below the image's bottom.

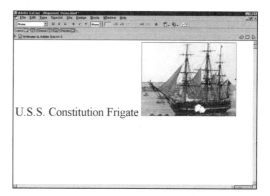

Left Alignment

Left alignment takes the image completely out of the line it was inserted into and makes it "float" to the next available space below the text on the left side of the page. If the image is in text that takes up more than one line, the image will drop to the left margin below the line that contains it and the other text will wrap around it on the right.

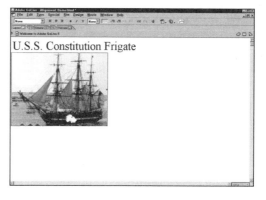

Right Alignment

Right alignment does the same thing as left alignment, but it floats the image to the next available space on the right side of the page.

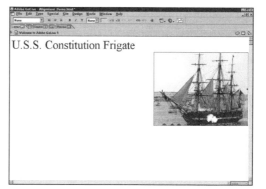

Text Top Alignment

Text Top alignment is essentially the same as Top alignment, except that the image is technically being aligned with the top of the text instead of the text being aligned with the top of the image.

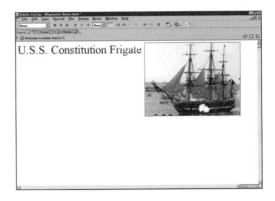

Abs Middle Alignment

Abs Middle alignment differs from Middle alignment in that it puts the middle of the text on an imaginary line through the middle of the image instead of using the baseline of the text. The main effect is that the text is slightly lower.

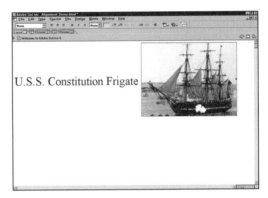

Baseline Alignment

Baseline alignment is the same as Bottom alignment.

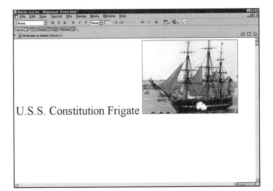

Abs Bottom Alignment

Abs Bottom alignment differs from Bottom alignment in that it doesn't use the baseline to align the text and image. Instead, it uses the absolute bottom part of the text—in this case, the letter "g" in the word "Frigate." If there are no letters that have parts below the baseline, this style is indistinguishable from Bottom alignment.

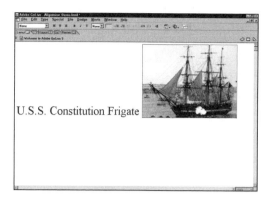

Multiple Alignments

When multiple images appear on one line, each one can have its own alignment. The second image has Text Top alignment, by the way, and is aligned to the top of the text. If it had Top alignment, it would line up with the top of the highest other element—the first image.

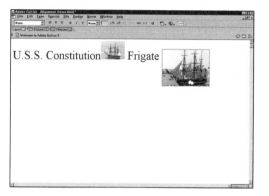

Working with Standard Alignment

It's easy to have an image on the left margin without floating it—just make it the first item on a line. What if you want to center an image, though? What if you want it on the right margin without floating it out of its surrounding text?

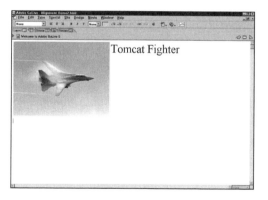

Centering

To center an image, just click anywhere within the paragraph that contains it and then click on the Center button in the toolbar. The entire paragraph will be centered.

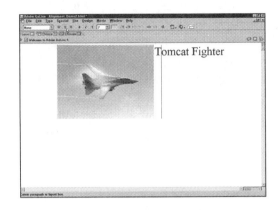

Right Aligning

Likewise, you can right align a paragraph that contains an image by clicking anywhere within it and then clicking on the Right button in the toolbar.

A standalone image can, of course, be centered or right aligned by the same method.

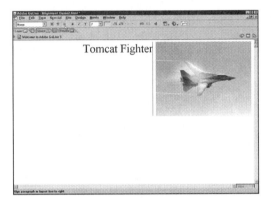

Viewing Alignment in HTML Source Code

The HTML source code shows that the alignment buttons work by encapsulating the selected element in a DIV element and then setting the DIV's align attribute.

```
<div align="right">
<p><font size="7">Tomcat Fighter</font>
<img src="conn-goldtom_400.jpg" width="400"
 height="300" border="0" align="texttop"></p>
</div>
```

Combining Alignments

You can combine both alignment methods. In this example, the paragraph containing the image was moved to the right margin via the toolbar button. The image was then given a Middle alignment via the Image Inspector to change the vertical alignment of the text.

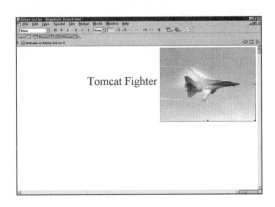

Combining Left and Right Alignments

The only exceptions to the combined alignment approach are the Left and Right image alignments in the Image Inspector. They will still float an image down to the next line after the one it's in and any text following that line will wrap around the image.

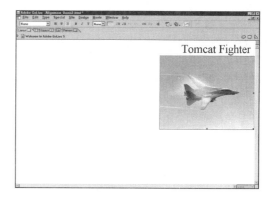

Framing the Picture

The use of borders around an image drifts in and out of style. Regardless of the popularity of borders, some images look better with them and others don't.

Using Borders

Sometimes, you have to use a border—for instance, image links are identified by the blue color of their border, just as text links are recognizable by their blue color and underlining.

See Chapter 6 for information on image links and text links.

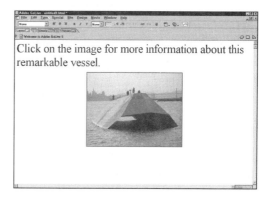

Setting Borders

To set a border, select the image and make sure the Border checkbox is selected. Next, enter a value in the Border text box.

Image borders are set in pixels.

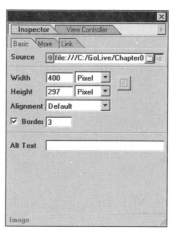

Adjusting Borders

A value of 1 leaves a barely visible border. A border value of at least 3 pixels and no more than 6 pixels is generally acceptable. Anything more than 6 pixels is usually considered to be overkill.

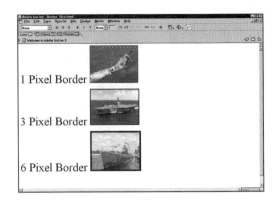

Setting Alternatives

Alt (alternative) text and *low resolution images* are placeholders that show while an image is downloading. They're less important as placeholders than they once were because high modem speeds, especially broadband, have made the wait negligible. If you have a lot of large image files, however, you should still use them. And alt text should be used in any case, because it has numerous other uses and not all programs show Web images.

Adding Alt Text

The HTML source code shows that alternative text is set as the value of the alt attribute.

```
<img src="glc0603b_400.jpg"
width="400" height="300" border="0"
alt="Submarine Museum">
```

1.

To set alt text, select the image and then click within the Alt Text box in the Image Inspector.

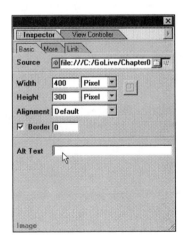

2.

Enter the descriptive text.

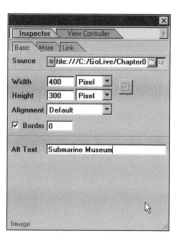

Alt text is not just an extra thing that you can do. To a blind person, it's critical to their understanding of your page. To a search engine, it may mean a difference in your ranking.

3.

The alt text will show up under several circumstances, including when the original image file becomes unavailable for any reason.

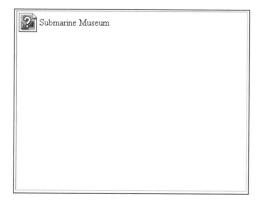

Adding Low Resolution Images

Low resolution images are typically black and white or grayscale. They give just enough visual information for a viewer to get an idea of what's coming when the full version appears.

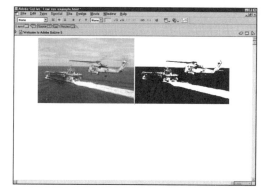

1.

Select the image, and then click on the More tab in the Image Inspector.

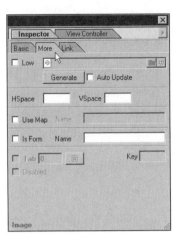

2.

Click on the Low checkbox. If you have created your own low resolution image in an external program such as Photoshop, Fireworks, or Paint Shop Pro, you can link it just as you would load a regular image—by using the Browse button or the point and shoot button.

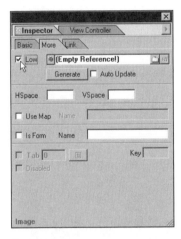

3.

If you don't have a low resolution image available, you can create one easily by clicking on the Generate button. GoLive will create a black-and-white version of the image in the same folder.

Click on the Auto Update checkbox if you want the low resolution version to change any time you change the main version.

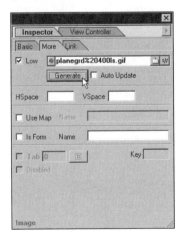

Resizing and Spacing Images

Sometimes, an image is just what you want, but it isn't quite the right size for a particular page design.

Changing Image Sizes

The secret to resizing images lies in the width and height attributes of the IMG element. Any change to their values changes the size of the image on the Web page.

```
<img src="Shuttle_Liftoff_200.jpg" width="200"
height="203" border="0">
```

Enlarging Images

Enlarging any bitmapped image like the ones that are used on the Web results in some blockiness—the larger the expansion, the blockier and more blurry the image becomes.

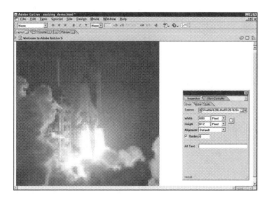

It's generally a good idea to do any image expansion in a professional quality graphics program.

Reducing Images

Reducing a large image, however, tends to sharpen the picture.

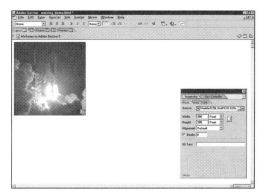

It is only the appearance of the image in a Web browser that is reduced; the file size remains the same.

Interactively Changing Image Sizes

To interactively change the size of a selected image, place your mouse pointer over the resizing handle at the bottom of the image. Press the mouse button and hold it down while you move the pointer up or down. When the size is right, release the mouse button. To change horizontal size, use the right handle. To change both directions at once, use the handle on the bottom right corner.

Changing the Image Size in the Image Inspector

To change the size in the Image Inspector, select the current value in the Width or Height box and type a new one over it.

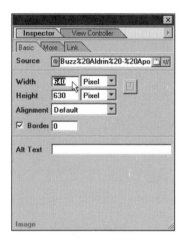

Proportionally Resizing Images

Unless you're looking for some bizarre effect, you probably want to proportionally resize the image. To do so, select Image from the drop-down list for either Width or Height.

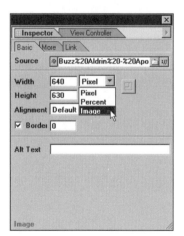

Returning Images to Original Size

Resizing in GoLive doesn't affect the original image file at all. To return a resized image to its original dimensions, select it and then click on the Reset Image Size button in the Image Inspector.

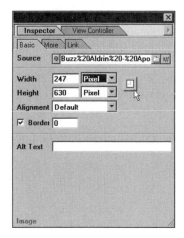

Adding Space around Images

You can put space around images in a variety of ways, of course—by adding nonbreaking spaces in front of or after an image or by adding line breaks above or below it. For real precision control, however, there are two settings—*HSpace* and *VSpace*.

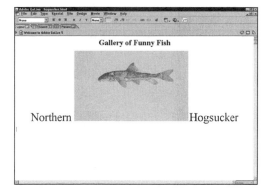

1.

Select an image and click on the More tab of the Image Inspector. Next, enter new values in one or both of the HSpace (horizontal space) and VSpace (vertical space) boxes.

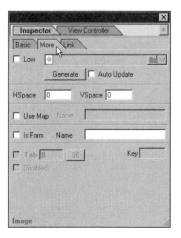

2.

HSpace adds space on both sides, and VSpace adds space both above and below the image. While the image is selected, a thin border shows in GoLive to represent the new spacing.

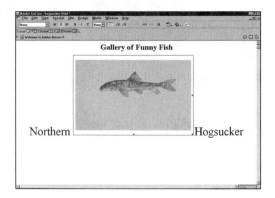

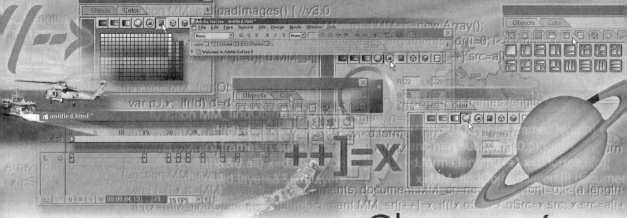

Chapter 6
Linking

- Using text and image links to connect Web pages

- Working with named anchors to move around a Web page

- Adding multiple links to your Web pages with image maps

Links Are the World (Wide Web)

If you understand nothing else about Web design, you must understand links. Links (also called hyperlinks) make the Web what it is. Without links, there couldn't even be a World Wide Web, because they're what enables you to move from page to page.

Adding Text Links

The most common type of link is the text link. By default, text links are differentiated from normal text by underlined, blue-colored characters.

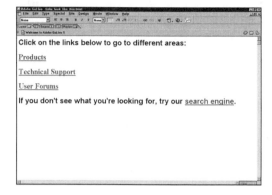

1.

Select the text that you want to make into a link.

You can select any amount of text, from a single character up to the entire Web page, for a single link. A link can consist of multiple paragraphs.

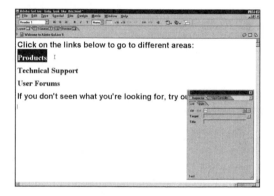

2.

In the Text Inspector, click on the Link button.

If the Text Inspector isn't open, choose Window|Inspector from the menu.

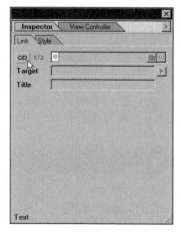

3.

The selected text immediately becomes a link, even though no value has been assigned to it yet.

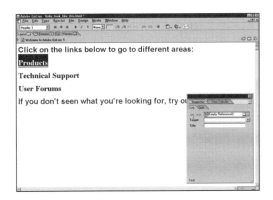

4.

The Link button in the Text Inspector grays out, and the Remove Link button becomes available. The link reference also activates.

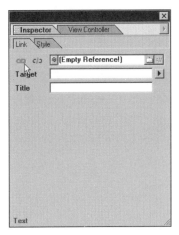

5.

Select the "(Empty Reference!)" placeholder and type the URL of the Web page or other file you want to link to. If you enter a URL that is outside your own site, the Absolute Link button will automatically depress itself.

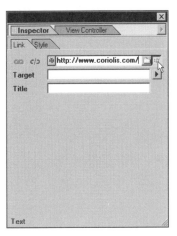

Adding a Link to Your Own Site

If the Web page or other file you want to link to is a part of your own site, you can use the point and shoot button in the Text Inspector to link to files that are listed in the Site Window.

See Chapter 2 for information on opening the Site Window.

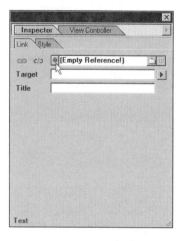

1.

The Layout area and the Site Window must be resized so that they are both accessible at the same time.

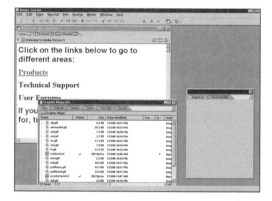

2.

Click on the point and shoot button and keep holding the mouse button down. Drag the pointing line to the name of the file you want to link to in the Site Window, and then release the mouse button.

If the Site Window is partially obscured by the Layout area (as in the preceding figure), it will come to the top.

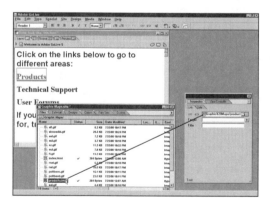

Adding a Link to a File on Your System

To create a link to a file on your system, either within or outside the site, click on the Browse button in the Text Inspector.

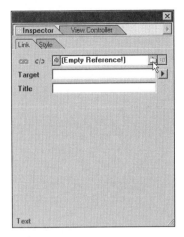

Navigate to the directory that contains the file you want to link to, and then double-click on the file name (or click on the file name and then click on the Open button).

Creating a Placeholder Link

If you want to create a placeholder link—one that does not have any file yet connected to it—select the text and click on the New Link button in the toolbar or in the Text Inspector.

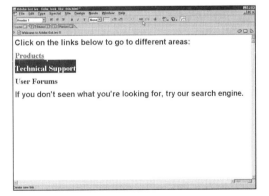

Adding a Text Link from a Web Browser

You can also insert a link from the Address or Location window of a Web browser. To do so, you first need to arrange GoLive and the Web browser so that both are visible. Next, click on the browser's Address icon.

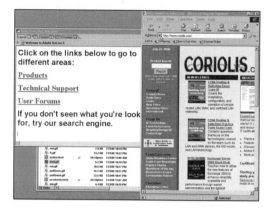

Drag the icon into GoLive and drop it on your Web page at the location where you want to create the link.

Netscape Navigator will drop only the URL itself. Internet Explorer will create a link whose text reads "Link."

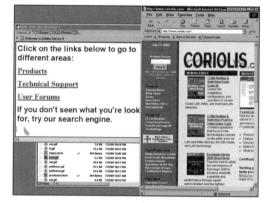

Using the Toolbar to Remove a Text Link

To remove a link, select it, and then click on the Remove Link button in the toolbar.

You can click on the New Link button, and then type the text for the link. When you're done and want to type normal text, click the Remove Link button and continue typing.

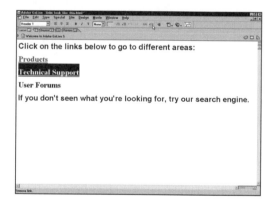

Using the Text Inspector to Remove a Text Link

You can also use the Remove Link button in the Text Inspector to remove a link from selected text.

Using Image Links

Words aren't the only way to make links between files. Any image can also be a link.

See Chapter 5 for information on using image files.

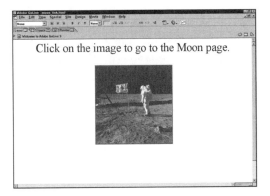

1.

To create an image link, you must first have an image selected.

Make sure that your image has a border. The borders of images used as links turn into the same color as text links.

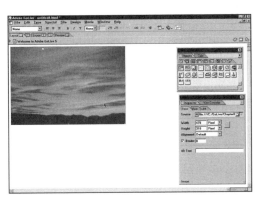

2.

Unlike with the Text Inspector, the Link buttons are not automatically displayed in the Image Inspector. Click on the Link tab to display the link information. From this point on, the process is identical to that for creating text links.

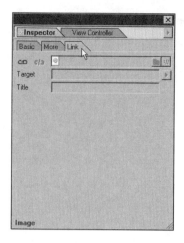

Working with Mailto Links

Mailto links can be either text- or image-based. The difference between them and normal links is that mailto links launch an email program to send a message instead of linking a Web browser to another file.

Click here to send mail to the Webmaster.

1.

Begin a text or image link in the same way as for a normal link. In the Inspector's Link tab, type the "mailto:" prefix followed by the email address you want to trigger a message to.

2.

When the mailto link is clicked on in a Web browser, the browser launches whatever email program its preferences are set for. The email program contains a blank message already addressed to the URL in the link.

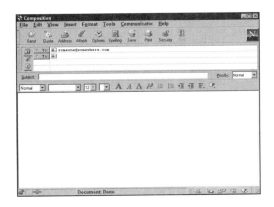

Working with Anchors

Links don't have to lead outside the Web page they're on. An anchor names a particular place on a Web page. You can use the name to jump from one part of a page to another specific place.

Marking Locations

One of the most common uses of anchors is to establish a link back to the top of the page on long Web pages.

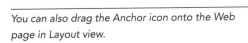

1.

Place your text cursor where you want to insert a named anchor. Then, on the Basics tab of the Objects palette, double-click the Anchor icon. An anchor icon appears on the Web page.

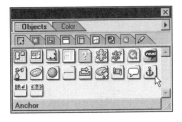

You can also drag the Anchor icon onto the Web page in Layout view.

2.

In the Anchor Inspector, the default name "anchor" appears. Highlight the name and type the name of your anchor over it.

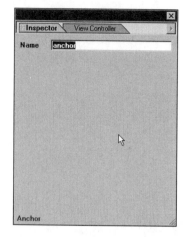

3.

To link to the anchor, create a link as you normally would, but stop at the point where you are ready to specify the URL. Next, click on the point and shoot button in the Text Inspector or Image Inspector and hold the mouse button down.

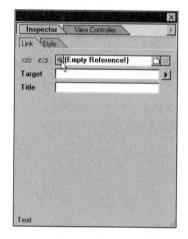

4.

Drag the line to the anchor in Layout view and release the mouse button.

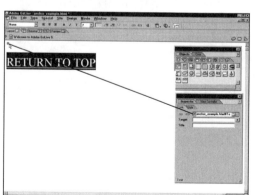

You can use point and shoot to create an anchor and link to it simultaneously. Just drag the line to the part of the page you want to anchor to.

Using Image Maps

Image maps are a kind of super image link. Although normal image links have only one URL per image, image maps can have an unlimited number of links keyed to a single image.

Adding Image Maps

The real trick is to pick an image that is intuitively comprehensible as a map. Sometimes you'll use something like a montage of product images, and sometimes you'll create a geographical map.

*Maps courtesy of **graphicmaps.com**.*

1.

Select an existing image on the Web page and click on the More tab in the Image Inspector. Click on the Use Map checkbox to select it. GoLive will create a map name based on the file name of the image.

See Chapter 5 for information on inserting images into Web pages.

2.

The toolbar changes to show GoLive's image mapping tools. From left to right, they are Select Region, Create Rectangle, Create Circle, Create Polygon, Display URLs, Frame Regions, Color Regions, and Select Color.

Creating a Rectangle Link Area

To draw a rectangular link area, click on the Create Rectangle button. Next, click on your image where you want one corner of the rectangle to be. While still holding down the mouse button, drag to the point where you want the opposite corner to be.

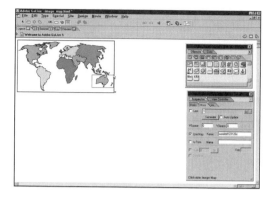

Release the mouse button. A colored, shaded area will cover the area where you drew the rectangle.

The shaded area will not appear on the image map in a Web browser.

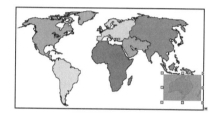

Creating a Circular Link Area

To draw a circular link area, click on the Create Circle button, and then click on your image where you want to put one edge of the circle. While still holding down the mouse button, drag to the point where you want the opposite edge to be.

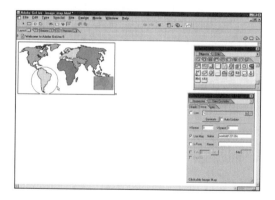

Release the mouse button. A colored, shaded area will cover the area where you drew the circle.

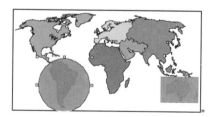

Creating a Polygon Link Area

To draw an irregularly shaped link area, click on the Create Polygon button, and then click on your image anywhere along the edge of the area you want to cover. Do not hold the mouse button down.

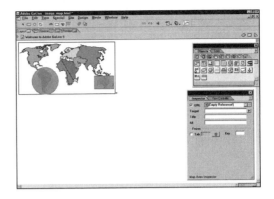

Click at more points along the edge until you have outlined the entire shape. When you have finished outlining the shape, click on the Select Region button.

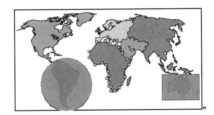

Setting a URL for any Shape

To set a URL for any of the three kinds of shapes to link to, select the shaded area. Next, in the Map Area Inspector, enter a URL the same way as you do for a normal link—by typing, by clicking on the Browse button, or by using point and shoot.

Modifying Image Maps

Sometimes a map area isn't precisely placed or sized. GoLive lets you move and resize the areas. The program also provides a few extras, such as the the ability to change the color of a shaded area.

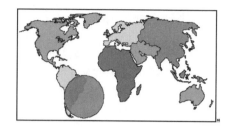

Moving a Map Area

To move a map area, click on the Select Region button. Next, place the mouse pointer over the area, press the mouse button, and drag the area into its new location. To drop it in its new place, release the mouse button.

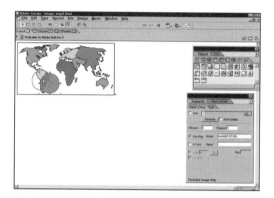

Resizing a Map Area

To resize a map area, click on the Select Region button. Next, click on one of the sizing handles that appear around the shape. Drag in the direction in which you want to expand or contract the area, and then release the mouse button.

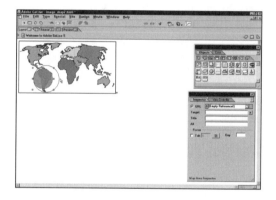

Working with Map Areas

Click on the Display URLs button to make visible the actual links assigned to each map area.

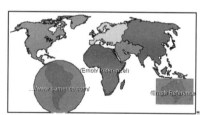

Like the area shading, this tool will be seen only while you are using GoLive; it will not show up on the image map in a Web browser.

Using the Frame Regions Button

The Frame Regions button is selected by default. Deselecting it leaves the regions colored, but without the thin border frame that delineates them while you work with them in GoLive.

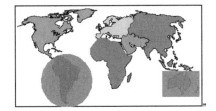

Using the Color Regions Button

The Color Regions button is selected by default. Deselecting it leaves the regions framed, but without the special color that marks them while you work with them in GoLive.

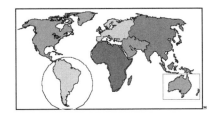

Working without the Frame Regions and Color Regions Buttons

When both the Frame Regions button and the Color Regions button are deselected, there is nothing to show where the map areas are. However, if you know where they are and click within one of them, it will still be marked by the sizing handles.

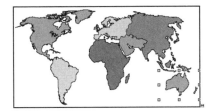

Adding Color

Click on the Select Color button to open the Color palette, where you can choose the color of the shaded map areas.

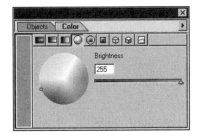

See Chapter 2 for a discussion of color options.

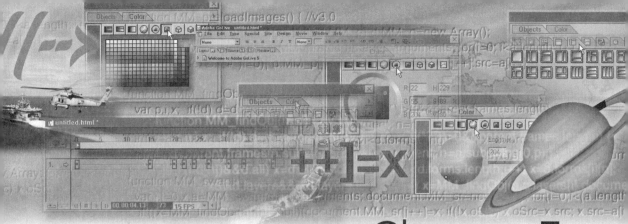

Chapter 7
Gathering Info with Forms

- Add forms to your Web pages and set the programs that will process their input

- Populate your forms with text boxes, radio buttons, checkboxes, and other controls

- Explore the different kinds of form buttons

Working with Forms

Forms are the number one method of getting input from Web visitors. The FORM element is built into HTML, and its purpose is to provide a place for gathering information that is then submitted to a program for processing.

Adding the Form

Forms and their constituent controls are found on the Forms tab of the Objects palette.

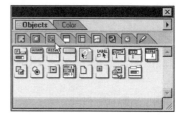

1.

Before you insert any form controls, you need to add the FORM element that will contain them. To do so, double-click on the Form icon or drag it from the Objects palette into the Layout area.

2.

The Form Inspector shows the default name "FormName." Highlight the default name and type a unique name for the form over it.

If the Form Inspector isn't showing, choose Window|Inspector from the menu.

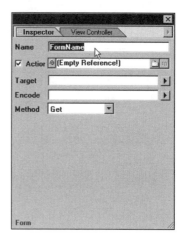

Action Field

The Action field is where you tell GoLive where to find the program that will be used to process the information that your site's visitors enter into the form controls. One method of doing that is to highlight the default entry, "(Empty Reference!)," and type the URL over it. If you enter a URL that is outside your own site, the Absolute Link button will automatically depress itself.

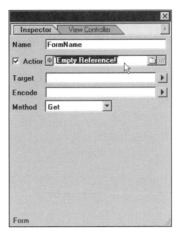

1.

If the program that processes the form input data is a part of your own site, you can use the point and shoot button in the Form Inspector to link to it.

See Chapter 2 for information on opening the Site Window.

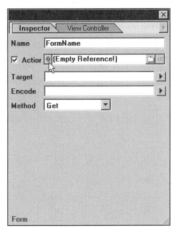

2.

The Layout area and the Site Window must be resized so that they are both accessible at the same time.

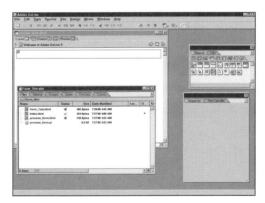

3.

Click on the point and shoot button and keep holding the mouse button down. Drag the pointing line to the name of the form data processing file in the Site Window, and then release the mouse button.

If the Site Window is partially obscured by the Layout area, it will come to the top.

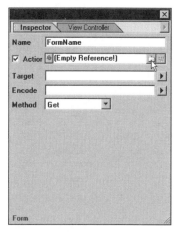

4.

To enter the location of a form data processing program on your system, either within or outside the site, click on the Browse button in the Form Inspector.

5.

Navigate to the directory that contains the form data processing file, and then double-click on the file name (or click on the file name and then click on the Open button).

Target Arrow

Enter the name of a target window in the Target box or click on the Target arrow to display a list of available targets.

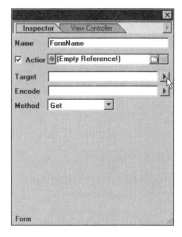

Encode Arrow

Click on the Encode arrow to choose from the list of available form data encoding formats. The three choices are Default, application/x-www-form-urlencoded, and multipart/form-data. The first two options are the same thing and are used for submitting normal ASCII information. For other types of data, use multipart/form-data.

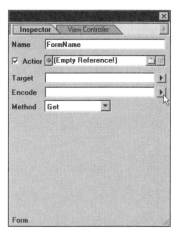

Method Arrow

Click on the Method arrow to view the list of methods. The choices are Default, Get, and Post. Default and Get are the same thing. The Get method sends form input by appending it to the URL specified in the Action attribute. The Post method sends form input separately, which means that more data can be sent with it than with the Get method.

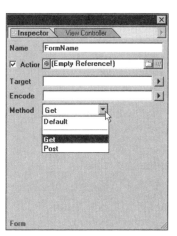

Working with Words

There are two kinds of input you can get from your site visitors—preprogrammed choices and freeform responses. When it comes to the latter, GoLive provides different ways to get textual responses from your visitors, and a couple more for you to use in your form design.

Adding Text and Password Fields

Text fields are small boxes for entering short amounts of text. Password fields are identical to text fields except for one thing—the text that is entered into a password field is displayed as asterisks.

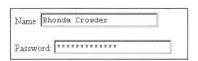

Text Field

To insert a text field, double-click on the Text Field icon in the Forms tab of the Objects palette. You can also drag the Text Field icon from the Objects palette into the form in the Layout area.

Password Field

To insert a password field, double-click on the Password icon in the Forms tab of the Objects palette. You can also drag the Password icon from the Objects palette into the form in the Layout area.

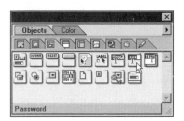

Name Field

The Form Text Field Inspector and Form Password Inspector are identical except for the words at the bottom. Highlight the default Name and enter one of your own.

If the Inspector isn't showing, choose Window|Inspector from the menu.

Value Field

The Value field is optional. Anything you enter here will appear in the text field as its
default value. You might, for example, enter
"1" as the value for a text field in an order
form to save users the trouble of entering anything unless they wanted to buy more than
one item.

Visible and Max Values

The Visible and Max values work together.
Visible sets the size of the text box that shows
in a Web browser. Max sets the maximum
number of characters that can be entered into
the text box. If no maximum value is set, there
is no limit on the number of characters, regardless of the physical size of the text box.

Is Password Field Checkbox

The Is Password Field checkbox is automatically selected for password fields, but not for
text fields. Clearing it changes the words at
the bottom of the Inspector from "Form Password" to "Form Text Field." Selecting it does
the reverse.

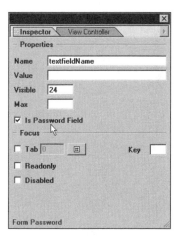

Readonly Checkbox

Select the Readonly checkbox if you have entered something in the Value field that you don't want form users to be able to change.

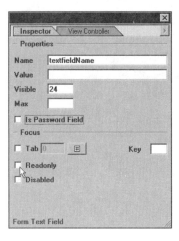

Adding Text Areas

Text areas are boxes that are used for larger text entries than will comfortably fit into a text field. You might use a text field to hold a name or an address, but it's not suitable for things such as comments or code samples.

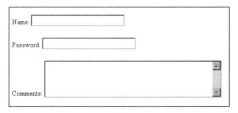

1.

To insert a text area, double-click on the Text Area icon in the Forms tab of the Objects palette. You can also drag the Text Area icon from the Objects palette into the form in the Layout area.

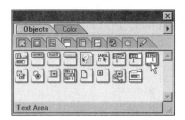

2.

The Form Text Area Inspector shows the default name "textareaName." Highlight the default name and type a unique name for the form over it.

If the Form Text Area Inspector isn't showing, choose Window|Inspector from the menu.

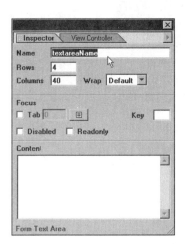

3.

Enter values for the Rows and Columns settings to set the size of the text area. Each row is one text line high, and each column is one character wide.

Wrap Options

Click on the Wrap arrow to choose the kind of word wrap you want. The options are Default, Off, Virtual, and Physical. Their interpretations vary from one Web browser to another.

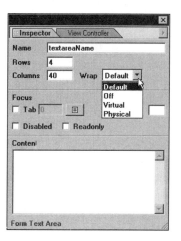

Internet Explorer and Wrap Options

In Internet Explorer, Default, Virtual, and Physical all wrap the text to the next line when it reaches the right edge of the text area. If the text extends below the bottom edge, vertical scrollbars will appear. The Off setting keeps all the text on one line, and sets up a scrollbar at the bottom.

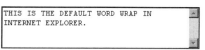

Default

Off

Virtual

THIS IS "PHYSICAL" WORD WRAP IN
INTERNET EXPLORER.

Physical

Netscape Navigator and Wrap Options

In Netscape Navigator, Default and Off are identical. Virtual and Physical wrap text at the right edge, just as Internet Explorer does.

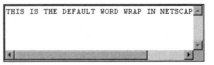

Default

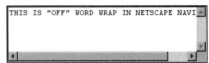

Off

Virtual

Physical

Readonly Checkbox

The Readonly checkbox is used in conjunction with the Content area. Like the Value field in text boxes, Content holds anything you want displayed by default in the text area. If the Readonly checkbox is selected, the content cannot be altered by form users.

Readonly does not work in Netscape Navigator.

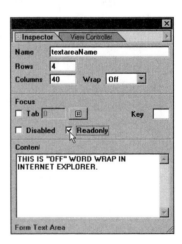

Adding Labels

Most form designers use plain text to describe form controls. However, if your audience is definitely composed solely of people using recent versions of Internet Explorer, you can use HTML labels instead. The only difference is that a user can click on the label instead of the control to activate the control.

1.

The Label element isn't useful unless there's already another form control in place to attach it to. The easiest way to use labels is to alternate inserting a form control and adding a label, inserting a form control and adding a label, and so forth.

2.

To insert a label, double-click on the Label icon in the Forms tab of the Objects palette. You can also drag the Label icon from the Objects palette into the form in the Layout area.

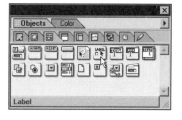

3.

After the label and its attendant form control are in place, it's time to connect the two.

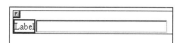

4.

The Form Label Inspector has a Reference text box, but you do not need to enter any value into it. Instead, use the point and shoot button to connect the label and its attendant form control.

If the Form Label Inspector isn't showing, choose Window|Inspector from the menu.

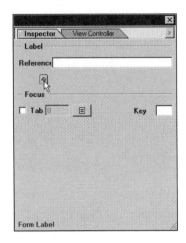

5.

Click on the point and shoot button. Hold the mouse button down and drag the line from the point and shoot button to the form control that you want to associate with the label. Release the button.

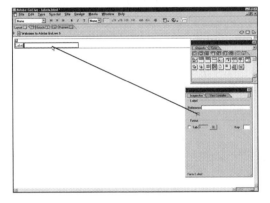

6.

Although you will see no indication in the Inspector for the form control, the HTML source code reveals that a particular ID has been established for the form control that the label refers to.

```
<label for="ID_textfieldName_1BFF7BF4141AAA0">
Label</label><input type="text"
name="textfieldName" size="24"
id="ID_textfieldName_1BFF7BF4141AAA0">
```

7.

There is no Value or Content field in the Form Label Inspector. To change the text of the label, you need to click within its boundaries and manually edit it.

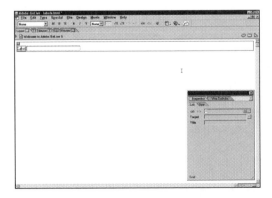

Adding Hidden Tags

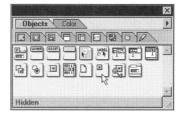

```
<input type="hidden" value="hiddenValue"
name="hiddenName">
```

There are really two kinds of read-only information. A text field, password field, or text area that is set to read-only is visible to the user, but a hidden tag is not visible at all. Hidden data can be used for such things as internal numbers that are not meaningful to outsiders.

1.

To insert a hidden tag, double-click on the Hidden icon in the Forms tab of the Objects palette. You can also drag the Hidden icon from the Objects palette into the form in the Layout area.

2.

In the Form Hidden Inspector, select the default value "hiddenName" and type over it to replace it with the name you need for your particular item.

If the Form Hidden Inspector isn't showing, choose Window|Inspector from the menu.

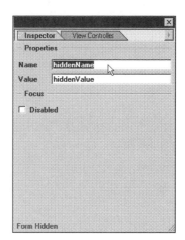

3.

Select the default value "hiddenValue" and type over it to replace it with the value you need for your particular item.

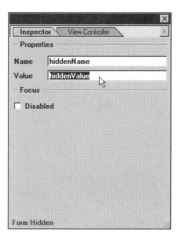

Presenting Choices

There are lots of choices that form users must make. GoLive makes it easy with list boxes, pop-up menus, checkboxes, and radio buttons.

Adding Pop-up Menus and List Boxes

Pop-up menus and list boxes are used to present many options in a small area. Although they appear different, they are both combinations of the SELECT and OPTION elements in standard HTML.

1.

To insert a pop-up menu, double-click on the Pop-up icon in the Forms tab of the Objects palette. You can also drag the Pop-up icon from the Objects palette into the form in the Layout area.

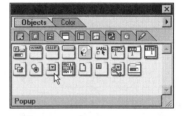

2.

To insert a list box, double-click on the List Box icon in the Forms tab of the Objects palette. You can also drag the List Box icon from the Objects palette into the form in the Layout area.

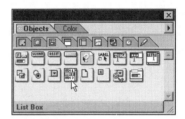

3.

The Form Pop-up Inspector and Form List Box Inspector are identical except for the words at the bottom. Highlight the default Name and enter one of your own.

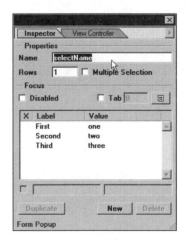

If the Inspector isn't showing, choose Window|Inspector from the menu.

4.

The number in the Rows box sets how many options are visible on a Web page. It is always 1 for a pop-up menu. Select the Multiple Selection checkbox if you are using a list box and want people to be able to choose more than one option.

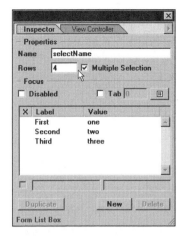

5.

GoLive shows placeholder labels and values. Click on one of them to activate the editing area below the Label/Value list. Next, select the text of the label or value you want to replace and type over it. To set a label as preselected, click on the checkbox at the beginning of the editing line.

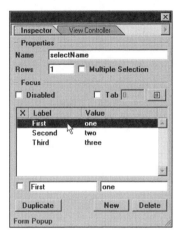

6.

Click on the New button to add a label/value pair. Select and type over the placeholders "item" and "value." Click on the Delete button to delete a selected label/value pair. Click on the Duplicate button to copy a selected label/value pair.

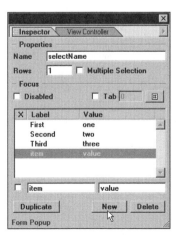

Adding Checkboxes

Checkboxes are used to present a small number of choices. Any number of checkboxes may be selected.

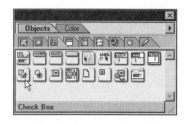

1.

To insert a checkbox, double-click on the Checkbox icon in the Forms tab of the Objects palette. You can also drag the Checkbox icon from the Objects palette into the form in the Layout area.

2.

In the Form Checkbox Inspector, highlight the default Name and type a unique name over it. Do the same for the default Value.

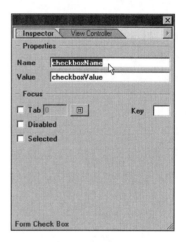

If the Form Checkbox Inspector isn't showing, choose Window|Inspector from the menu.

Adding Radio Buttons

Like checkboxes, radio buttons are used to offer only a few choices. Radio buttons, however, are mutually exclusive—if one is selected, all others in its group are automatically deselected.

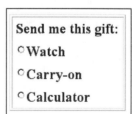

1.

To insert a radio button, double-click on the Radio Button icon in the Forms tab of the Objects palette. You can also drag the Radio Button icon from the Objects palette into the form in the Layout area.

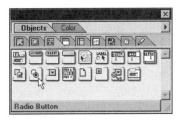

2.

In the Form Radio Button Inspector, highlight the default Group and type a unique name over it. If you have already assigned a group to one or more radio buttons, click on the arrow to open a list of available group names. Highlight the default Value and type a new value over it.

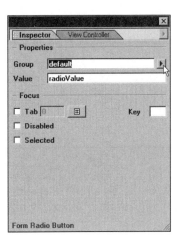

If the Form Radio Button Inspector isn't showing, choose Window|Inspector from the menu.

Understanding Buttons

GoLive presents a potentially bewildering variety of buttons to put on your forms. In this section, we show you how to use all five of them.

Adding Submit, Reset, and Normal Buttons

The Submit and Reset buttons are standard parts of almost all forms. Users click on the Submit button to send the data they have entered into the form. The Reset button clears all entries from the form. The Normal button has no preprogrammed function, so it can be used to trigger a custom script that performs some other action.

Submit Button

To insert a Submit button, double-click on the Submit Button icon in the Forms tab of the Objects palette. You can also drag the Submit Button icon from the Objects palette into the form in the Layout area.

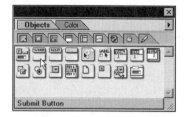

Reset Button

To insert a Reset button, double-click on the Reset Button icon in the Forms tab of the Objects palette. You can also drag the Reset Button icon from the Objects palette into the form in the Layout area.

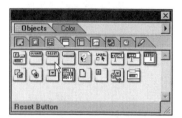

Form Button Inspector

In the Form Button Inspector, the three radio buttons allow you to choose another type of button if you change your mind after your initial selection. If you have more than one Submit button, highlight the default Name and type a unique name over it. If you don't want the button to read "Submit Query," click on the Label checkbox and type in new text.

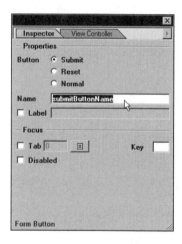

If the Form Button Inspector isn't showing, choose Window|Inspector from the menu.

Form Button Inspector for Reset Button

The Form Button Inspector for the Reset button is virtually identical to the standard Form Button Inspector, except that the Name option is grayed out. You can still click on the Label checkbox if you want to change the wording on the button, however.

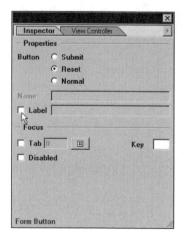

Normal Button

There is no icon in the Objects palette for the Normal button. To create one, insert either a Submit button or Reset button, and then click on the Normal radio button in the Form Button Inspector. Enter a unique Name, and then click on the Label checkbox and type the new label into the Label text box.

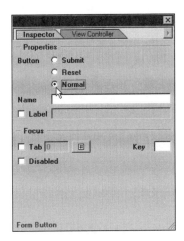

Adding Universal Buttons

There's not much in GoLive that's easier than getting confused about Normal and Universal buttons. The default labels for both simply say "Button," and the Form Button Inspector for each is virtually identical. Universal buttons, however, allow you to format the label.

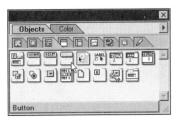

1.

To insert a Universal button, double-click on the Button icon in the Forms tab of the Objects palette. You can also drag the Button icon from the Objects palette into the form in the Layout area.

2.

The three radio buttons at the top of the Form Button Inspector have no effect in this case. Highlight the default Name and type a unique name over it. Enter a value in the Value text box.

If the Form Button Inspector isn't showing, choose Window|Inspector from the menu.

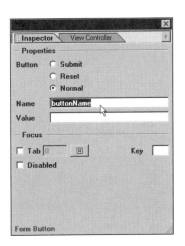

3.

To edit the label, click within the outlined area that holds the word "Button" in the center of the Universal button.

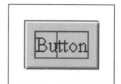

4.

Not only can you edit the label, but also you can apply any type of text style to it, including font size.

Adding Graphical Buttons

The Input Image is a Submit button that allows you to add your own graphical image for form users to click on instead of the standard Submit button.

1.

To insert an Input Image, double-click on the Form Input Image icon in the Forms tab of the Objects palette. You can also drag the Form Input Image icon from the Objects palette into the form in the Layout area.

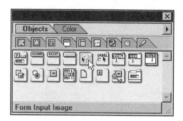

2.

The Form Input Image Inspector is the same as a normal Image Inspector (see Chapter 5). After you have indicated the source for the image to be used on the button, click on the More tab.

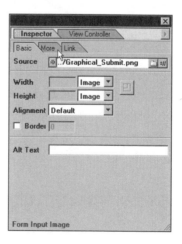

3.

The Is Form checkbox is selected by default. Click in the Name text box and enter a unique name for the Input Image.

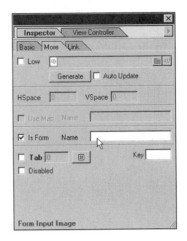

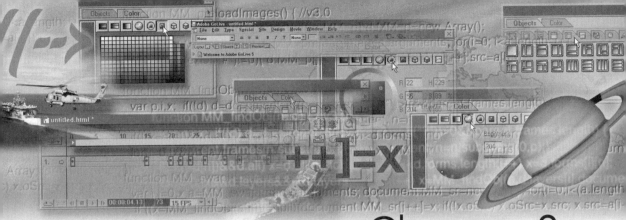

Chapter 8
Organizing with Tables

- Use tables to contain all the other elements on a Web page

- Change the size of tables, cells, rows, and columns to suit your needs

- Set individual cells to span several rows and/or columns

- Import existing table data into HTML formats

Working with Tables

Everything in HTML works on a container basis—one element contains other elements that, in turn, contain other elements, and so on. Tables make the relationship of the container and the contained visible and obvious.

Adding Tables

A table is a collection of boxes called *cells* that are arranged in rows and columns. The individual cells are used to contain other elements, such as text or images.

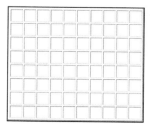

1.

To insert a table, place your text cursor where you want the table to appear, and then double-click on the Table icon in the Basic tab of the Objects palette. You can also drag the Table icon into the Layout area.

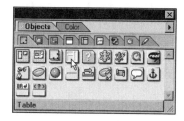

2.

The default table in GoLive is three columns across by three rows high (3×3).

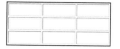

3.

In the Table Inspector, highlight the default numbers in the Rows and Columns text boxes and type your own values over them.

If the Table Inspector isn't showing, choose Window|Inspector from the menu.

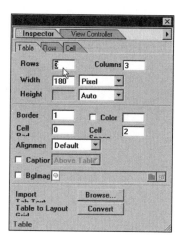

Resizing Tables

The default 3×3 table is only 180 pixels wide and 75 pixels high. You can resize the table through the Table Inspector settings. If you prefer working visually, tables can be resized by interactively dragging the borders.

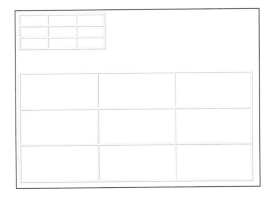

Resizing Using Pixels

To set a precise width in pixels, select the default value in the Width text box and type a new value over it.

The settings for Height values work exactly like those for Width values.

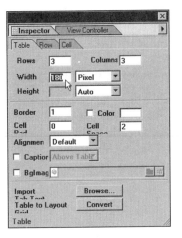

Resizing Using Percentages

To set the table width as a percentage of the Web page's width, click on the Width drop-down list and choose Percent. Next, enter the percentage value in the Width text box.

You must do it in this order. If you do it the other way around, GoLive will take the value as pixels, and then reset the percentage to equal that pixel size.

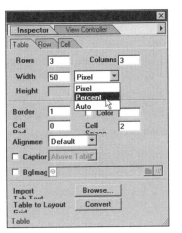

Resizing Automatically

Choose Auto from the Width drop-down list if you want to leave it up to the Web browser to automatically set the appropriate width for your table. The Width text box grays out if you choose Auto.

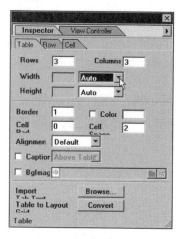

Resizing a Row

The width of a row is determined by the width of the table, so the only resizing option on the Row tab of the Table Inspector is Height. It works just like the settings for the table as a whole, except that the Percent option sets the row's height as a percentage of the table's height.

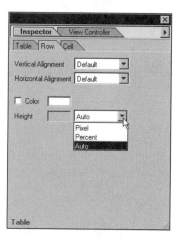

Resizing a Cell

The Cell tab of the Table Inspector provides both Width and Height value settings. As with rows, the Percent option sets the width or height of a cell as a percentage of the table's width or height.

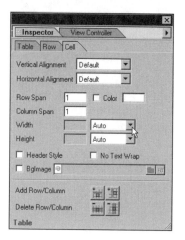

Changing Table Width with the Mouse

To change the width of a table, place the mouse pointer over the right border of the table. Press the Alt key (Option key on Macs) and the left mouse button. While holding the mouse button down, drag to the right to increase the width or to the left to decrease it.

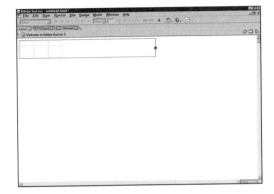

Changing Table Height with the Mouse

To change the height of a table, place the mouse pointer over the bottom border of the table. Press the Alt key (Option key on Macs) and the left mouse button. While holding the mouse button down, drag down to increase the height or up to decrease it.

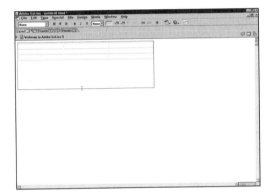

Adding and Deleting Rows and Columns

The number of rows and columns in the table can be changed by using a combination of the basic settings and a handful of buttons.

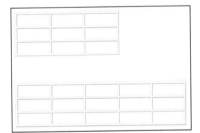

Using the Rows and Columns Settings

Rows and columns can be added or removed by changing the values in the Rows and Columns settings of the Table tab of the Table Inspector.

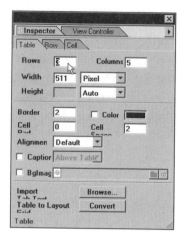

Adding Rows and Columns with the Rows and Columns Settings

Rows and columns added in this manner are limited by the following restrictions: All added rows are tacked onto the bottom of the table, and all added columns go onto the right side.

1A	2A	3A	4A	5A
1B	2B	3B	4B	5B
1C	2C	3C	4C	5C

Deleting Rows and Columns with the Rows and Columns Settings

When rows and columns are deleted by changing the Row and Column values, it is always the rightmost column(s) and lowest row(s) that are deleted.

1A	2A	3A	4A
1B	2B	3B	4B

Adding and Deleting with the Button Method

To add a row or column using the button method, you first need to select a cell by clicking on its right or bottom border.

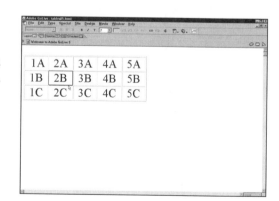

1.

Click on the Cell tab of the Table Inspector. The four buttons at the bottom of this tab are used to add and delete rows and columns. The first button adds a row. The second adds a column. The third deletes a row. The fourth deletes a column.

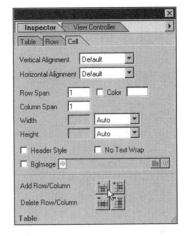

2.

Rows added by the button method go in above the row that contains the selected cell. Columns go in to the left of the column that contains it. The Delete buttons remove the row or column that contains the selected cell.

1A	2A	3A	4A	5A
1B	2B	3B	4B	5B
1C	2C	3C	4C	5C

Managing Cell Content

Of course, tables are meant to hold things like text, numbers, and images. But there's more to it than just typing or dragging in an image icon. You can control a lot of factors that will affect the appearance of your tables.

Adding Content

Table cells can hold much more than just words and numbers. They can contain anything you can put onto a regular Web page—including other tables.

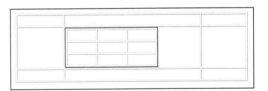

Adding Text

To add text to a table, click within a cell and begin typing. You can also paste text that you have copied from another program, another Web page, or another part of the same Web page. The cell will expand as content is entered. Tab to the next cell and repeat.

First Cell

Adding Objects

Objects from the various palettes can be dragged and dropped into the desired table cell. Copied objects also can be pasted into it.

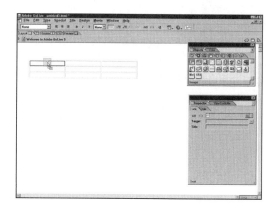

Choosing Cell Content

Careful planning is needed when choosing cell content. Because cells expand to accommodate the size of their contents, a single cell can radically alter the entire table.

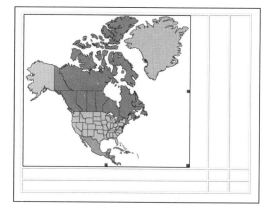

Importing Tabular Data

Tables were originally intended simply to display rows and columns of words and numbers, and GoLive has a special feature for importing existing tabular data. The data has to be in a delimited format such as tab-separated values (TSV) or comma-separated values (CSV).

Title	Author	Topic
The Gurkhas	Byron Farwell	History
The Spiritual Universe	Fred Alan Wolf	Physics
The Dance of Inner Peace	Rosalee Sirgany	Spirituality
Stand On Zanzibar	John Brunner	Science Fiction

1.

Select an empty table by clicking on its top or left border.

If there are any cells with content, the imported content will not overwrite it, but will be appended to it.

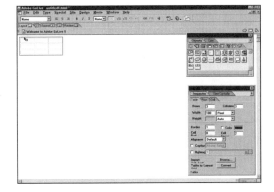

2.

Click on the Browse button near the bottom of the Table tab in the Table Inspector.

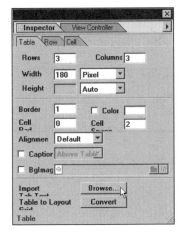

3.

Navigate to the directory that holds the data file you want to import.

The file must end in ".txt" or it cannot be imported. If the file has another extension, rename it before you attempt to import it.

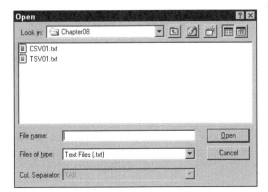

4.

Select the file. The Col. Separator drop-down list at the bottom of the Open dialog box activates.

Do not just double-click on the file name unless you are sure it's a tab-delimited file. If you do, and it isn't, the data may not be imported correctly.

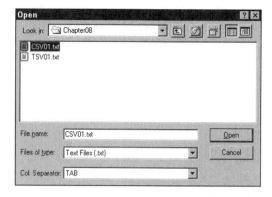

5.

Click on the Col. Separator drop-down list and select the type of column separator that the file you are importing uses. The default is tab separated. You can also choose commas, spaces, or semicolons as the delimiters. Click on the Open button to finish importing the file.

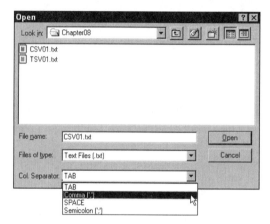

6.

The data from the file is imported and laid out in the table. The columns widen only to the extent of the longest word (or number) in the data. You must resize the table if you want everything to fall neatly onto single lines.

You can also apply text formatting to the data to improve its appearance.

Title	Author	Topic
The Gurkhas	Byron Farwell	History
The Spiritual Universe	Fred Alan Wolf	Physics
The Dance of Inner Peace	Rosalee Sirgany	Spirituality
Stand On Zanzibar	John Brunner	Science Fiction

Borders, Padding, and Spacing

Borders are the walls of cells and tables. Cell padding sets how much space is between the walls of the cell and its content. Cell spacing sets how far apart the cells are from one another. The default cell spacing is only two pixels, and the default cell padding is nothing at all.

Title	Author	Topic
The Gurkhas	Byron Farwell	History
The Spiritual Universe	Fred Alan Wolf	Physics
The Dance of Inner Peace	Rosalee Sirgany	Spirituality
Stand On Zanzibar	John Brunner	Science Fiction

Changing Border Thickness

To change the thickness of the border, select the value in the Border text box and type a new value over it. To change cell padding and cell spacing values, do the same in the Cell Pad and Cell Space text boxes.

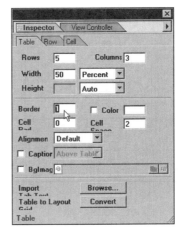

Changing Border Size

Changing the border size (in this case to 10 pixels) does not affect the borders around cells, only the major border around the entire table.

Title	Author	Topic
The Gurkhas	Byron Farwell	History
The Spiritual Universe	Fred Alan Wolf	Physics
The Dance of Inner Peace	Rosalee Sirgany	Spirituality
Stand On Zanzibar	John Brunner	Science Fiction

Setting Border Size to Zero

Changing the border size to zero, however, does affect the borders around the cells—it removes them, as well as the external table border.

Title	Author	Topic
The Gurkhas	Byron Farwell	History
The Spiritual Universe	Fred Alan Wolf	Physics
The Dance of Inner Peace	Rosalee Sirgany	Spirituality
Stand On Zanzibar	John Brunner	Science Fiction

Cell walls will still show up in Layout view, but not in a Web browser.

Increasing Cell Padding

Increasing cell padding (to six pixels in this example) increases readability by moving the contents away from the cell walls. It can, however, cause a word wrap because it effectively makes the cell's content area smaller.

Title	*Author*	*Topic*
The Gurkhas	Byron Farwell	History
The Spiritual Universe	Fred Alan Wolf	Physics
The Dance of Inner Peace	Rosalee Sirgany	Spirituality
Stand On Zanzibar	John Brunner	Science Fiction

Increasing Cell Spacing

Increasing cell spacing (to 10 pixels in this example) doesn't usually add much to the table's appearance.

Title	*Author*	*Topic*
The Gurkhas	Byron Farwell	History
The Spiritual Universe	Fred Alan Wolf	Physics
The Dance of Inner Peace	Rosalee Sirgany	Spirituality
Stand On Zanzibar	John Brunner	Science Fiction

Row and Column Span

Many times, a simple "one cell to a row or column" table just won't do the job. That's where row spanning and column spanning come into play to allow a single cell to take up the space of two or more cells.

Transportation Types					
Land		Sea		Air	
Trucks	Cars	Ships	Boats	Airplanes	Helicopters

1.

To set the span properties for a cell, select the cell by clicking on its right or bottom border.

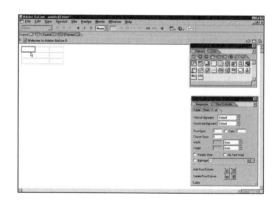

2.

Click on the Cell tab in the Table Inspector.

It's best to work with empty tables when setting cell span. If adjacent cells both have content and you change the cell span of one, you will delete the content of any cells to its right or below it.

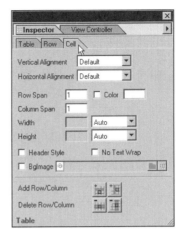

3.

To make a cell go across more than one row, highlight the current value in the Row Span text box and type a new value over it. To make a cell go across more than one column, do the same with the Column Span value.

GoLive will not let you set cell spanning values greater than the size of the table.

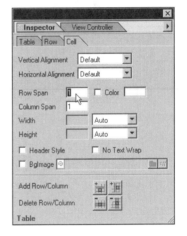

Adding Background Color and Images

Background color and background images in tables apply to cells only. Neither the border nor the space between cells is affected by these settings.

1.

To set the background color for all the cells in an entire table, select the table by clicking on its top or left border.

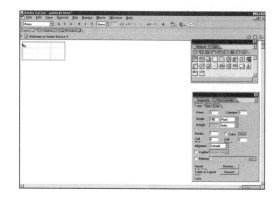

2.

In the Table Inspector, click on the Color checkbox so that it is selected, and then click on the Color box to open the Color palette.

See Chapter 2 for details on how to use color in GoLive.

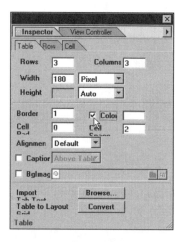

3.

To set a background image for all the cells in the table, click on the BgImage checkbox. Next, use the point and shoot button or the Browse button to select the image file to be used for the background.

See Chapter 5 for details on selecting image files.

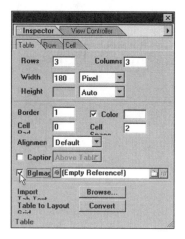

Setting Color for Rows

The Row tab also allows color to be set separately for a given row in the table. It has no background image option; if you want one, you'll have to manually enter the code for it. Background color for a row overrides the background color for the table.

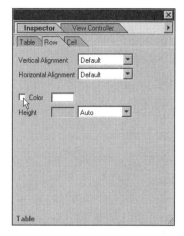

Setting Color for Cells

The Cell tab has both background color and background image options available. Background color and background image settings for individual cells override the same settings for a table or row.

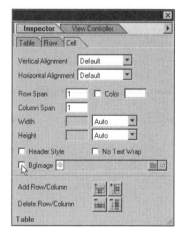

Working with Alignment

Tables are left aligned by default, but you can change the alignment for a table, a row, or an individual cell.

Title	Author	Topic
The Gurkhas	Byron Farwell	History
The Spiritual Universe	Fred Alan Wolf	Physics
The Dance of Inner Peace	Rosalee Sirgany	Spirituality
Stand On Zanzibar	John Brunner	Science Fiction

Aligning the Entire Table

To set alignment for an entire table, select it by clicking on its top or left border.

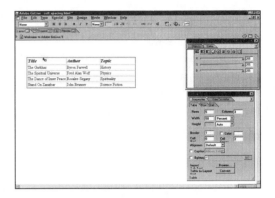

In the Table Inspector, click on the Alignment drop-down menu and choose Default, Left, or Right.

For overall alignment, default is the same as left alignment on all major Web browsers.

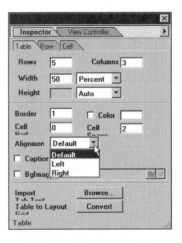

Aligning a Row or Cell

To set the alignment for a row or cell, select a cell by clicking on its bottom or right border.

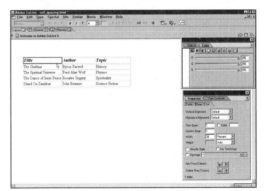

1.

In either the Row tab or the Cell tab, click on the Vertical Alignment drop-down list and select Default, Top, Middle, or Bottom.

For vertical alignment, default is the same as bottom alignment on all major Web browsers.

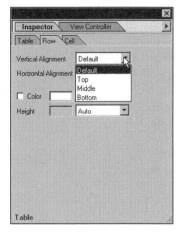

2.

In either the Row tab or the Cell tab, click on the Horizontal Alignment drop-down list and select Default, Left, Right, or Center.

For horizontal alignment, default is the same as left alignment on all major Web browsers.

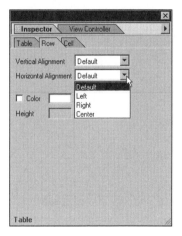

Using the Table Palette

In addition to the Table Inspector, GoLive offers another way to manage tables—the Table palette. This palette handles table styles and data sorting.

Applying Preformatted Styles

When it comes to dressing up a table, you can go through the laborious process of manually setting styles for all the text and the background colors, or you can let GoLive do it for you.

Title	Author	Topic
The Gurkhas	Byron Farwell	History
The Spiritual Universe	Fred Alan Wolf	Physics
The Dance of Inner Peace	Rosalee Sirgany	Spirituality
Stand On Zanzibar	John Brunner	Science Fiction

1.

To open the Table palette, choose Window|
Table from the menu.

---

*The tabs in the Table palette are prime candidates
for customization. Many people think that the Table
palette tabs should be part of the Table Inspector.
You can make them so by dragging the tabs from the
Table palette into the Table Inspector. See Chapter 1
for details on moving tabs.*

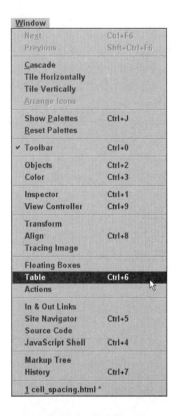

2.

In the Table palette, click on the Style tab.

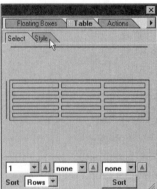

3.

Click on the drop-down list and select one of the built-in table styles.

If you want to see the kind of information that's stored with these styles, check out Styles.xml. In a standard Windows installation, it's found in the C:\Program Files\Adobe\GoLive 5.0_ENG\ Modules\TableStyles folder.

4.

A sample of the selected style is shown in the Table palette. To use that style on the selected table, click on the Apply button. To remove the style, click on the Clear button.

The Clear button clears all styles, including those you manually applied before using the Table palette.

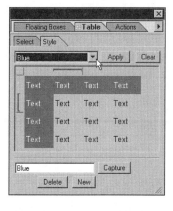

5.

Click on the Capture button to add the styles from a selected table to the list in the Table palette. Be cautious when capturing a style; it will take the place of whatever style is currently selected in the Table palette.

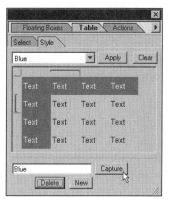

Creating New Styles

To safely create a new style based upon an existing table, first click on the New button. The word "New" will be added to the name of the style in the text box ("Orange" will become "New Orange," for example). Next, select the style name in the text box and type a new name over it.

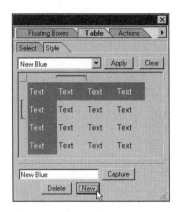

Deleting Existing Styles

To delete an existing style, select it from the drop-down list and then click on the Delete button.

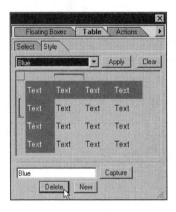

If you delete a style, the change is permanent, even for the default styles. You cannot undo the deletion.

Sorting

Table data isn't always in the order we'd like it to be. GoLive solves this problem by letting you sort the data of selected tables by columns.

Title	Author	Topic
The Gurkhas	Byron Farwell	History
The Spiritual Universe	Fred Alan Wolf	Physics
The Dance of Inner Peace	Rosalee Sirgany	Spirituality
Stand On Zanzibar	John Brunner	Science Fiction

1.

In the Table palette, click on the Select tab. The diagram in the Select tab will reflect the number of rows and columns in the selected table.

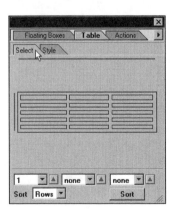

If the Table palette isn't open, choose Window|Table from the menu.

2.

Click on the Sort button to change the default "Sort Ascending" to "Sort Descending."

3.

Click on the Sort drop-down list and select either rows or columns to sort on.

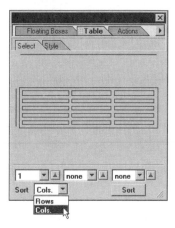

4.

For secondary columns or rows, choose which one to base the sort on. If no secondary sort is required, choose "none."

Continue to do the same for successive rows and columns.

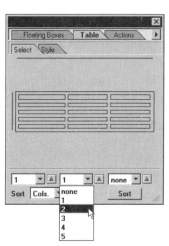

Using Layout Grids

Layout grids are a special sort of table that GoLive provides for laying out Web pages. This saves you the trouble of using tables to lay out individual Web pages yourself.

Creating a Layout Grid

Existing tables that have been used for layout purposes on Web pages can be converted to layout grids by selecting them and then clicking on the Convert button.

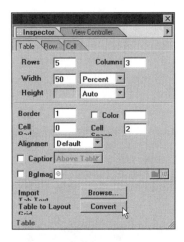

Creating a Layout Grid from Scratch

To create a layout grid from scratch, double-click on the Layout Grid icon in the Basic tab of the Objects palette. You can also drag the Layout Grid icon into the Layout area.

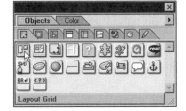

Resizing the Layout Grid

In the Layout Grid Inspector, you can set the width and height of the overall grid, as well as the size of the grid squares. Click on the Snap checkboxes to deselect them so that inserted objects do not snap to the lines. Enter new values in the Horizontal and Vertical text boxes to change the size of the grid. Deselect the Visible checkboxes to make the gridlines not show.

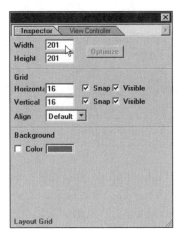

Aligning the Layout Grid

Just as with a normal table, you can set the alignment to Default, Left, or Right. You can also set a background color for the entire table by clicking on the Color checkbox and then on the Color text box.

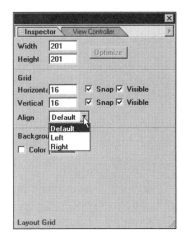

Default alignment is the same as left alignment in all major Web browsers.

Inserting a Text Cell in the Layout Grid

To insert a table cell that will contain text, double-click on the Layout Text Box icon in the Basic tab of the Objects palette. You can also drag the Layout Text Box icon into the Layout Grid.

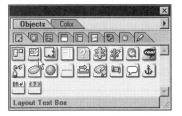

Using the Layout Text Box Inspector

The Layout Text Box Inspector offers fewer options than a normal Table Cell Inspector does. All you can do is set the background color and choose whether to allow content to overflow the bounds of the text box.

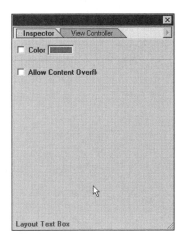

Chapter 9
Using Frames

- Use frame sets to display several files at once

- Add or delete frames to make GoLive's default frame sets cover all the possibilities

- Modify frame sets to suit your own needs

Displaying Multiple Files

Frames are a way to show two or more Web pages in a browser at the same time. It's perfectly possible to have the pages be totally unconnected in any way, or even to display files other than HTML files. You could, for example, have a pair of frames with one frame showing an image file and the other showing a Web page. However, the overwhelming majority of Web designers use frames for navigational purposes: A links page in one frame controls which Web page (or other file) is shown in the other window.

Creating a Frame Set

Although most framed pages are done in pairs (left and right or top and bottom), the number of frames is not technically limited. It's merely a matter of design and functionality.

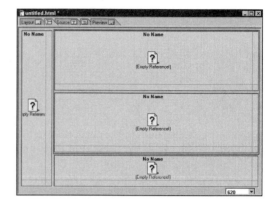

1.

Frames are not done in the Layout Editor, but in the Frames Editor, so you need to click on the Frames Editor tab before you can get started. At first, the Frames Editor is just a gray blank that reads "No Frames" in the center.

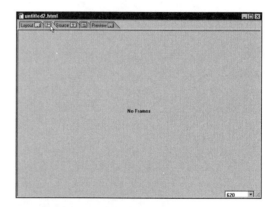

2.

Click on the Frames tab of the Objects palette. The first icon is used to add a single frame to an existing frame set. The rest are frame sets with two or three frames each.

3.

Click on a Frame Set icon and drag it into the Frames Editor.

You cannot double-click on a Frame Set icon to add it to the Frames Editor.

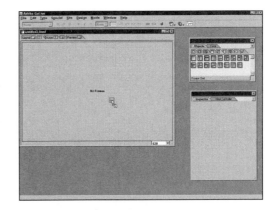

4.

An empty frame set appears. At the top of each frame are the words "No Name." In the center of each frame are a page icon and an "(Empty Reference!)" notation.

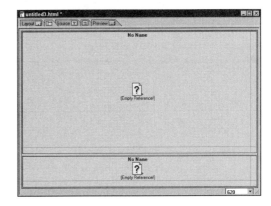

Selecting Frame Sets and Frames

To select a frame set, click on the border between two of its frames. To select an individual frame, click within the frame.

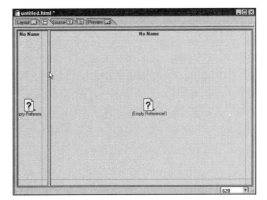

Using the Frame Set Size Option

In the Frame Set Inspector, the Size option is grayed out unless you are working with a nested frame set, which is one frame set placed inside another one.

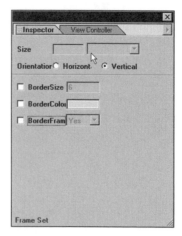

Frame sets can be only columns or rows. Any icon in the Frames tab of the Objects palette that has a mixture of rows and columns uses nested frame sets.

Choosing the Sizing Method

If the Size option is available, click on the drop-down list. Choose Pixel to set an exact size or Percent to set the size as a percentage of the containing frame; enter the desired value in the Size text box. Choose Scale to let GoLive set the size of all frames in the frame set equal to one another.

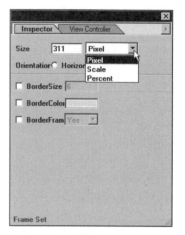

Changing a Frame Set's Orientation

You can change a row-oriented frame set to a column-oriented one, and vice versa, by clicking on the Horizontal or Vertical radio buttons.

Customizing Borders

The borders that divide the frames can be customized in several ways. If you wish to specify a size for the borders that divide the frames, click on the BorderSize checkbox and enter a value in the text box.

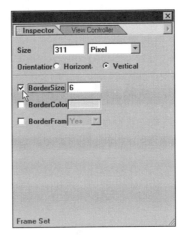

Changing Border Color

To specify a border color (gray is the default), click on the BorderColor checkbox, and then click in the color box.

For details on setting colors in GoLive, see Chapter 2.

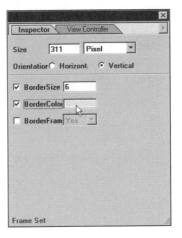

Eliminating Borders

If you do not want visible borders between the frames, click on the BorderFrame checkbox and select No from the drop-down list.

If you don't also change the border size to zero, you will have a blank space between the frames where the border used to be.

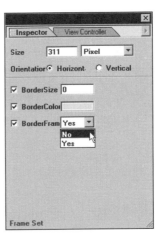

Adding Frame Content

Most of the time, one frame has unchanging content consisting of a set of links that determine which Web pages get displayed in another frame.

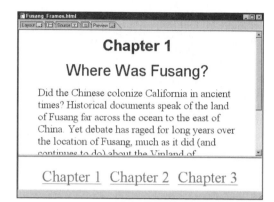

1.

Click within the frame you want to populate.

Even if the frame is a target—one that will host changing content—it should start out with something in it rather than being left blank.

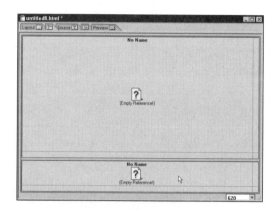

2.

In the Frame Inspector, highlight the default name and type a new name over it.

You don't have to name a frame unless you plan to use it as a target, but if you don't name each frame, you may have a confusing time trying to sort out the different ones that are all named "No Name."

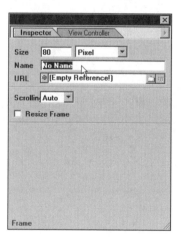

3.

Enter the URL of the file you want to put into the frame by typing it in, by using the point and shoot button, or by using the Browse button. You have to click on the Preview button to view the pages—the Frames Editor shows only file references.

See Chapter 6 for information on how to link to a file.

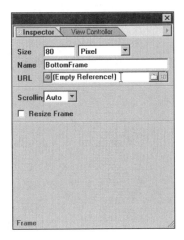

Adding and Deleting Frames

The default frame sets found in the Frames tab cover most of the layouts you are likely to need. However, GoLive is flexible enough that you can modify the basic setups to handle any situation.

Adding Frames

It's as easy to add frames in GoLive as it is to add frame sets, but you need to look out for a couple of "gotchas."

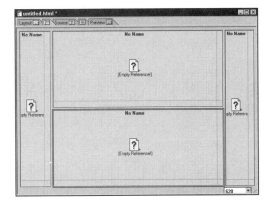

1.

To add a frame to an existing frame set, drag the Frame icon from the Frames tab of the Objects palette into one of the frames in the Frames Editor.

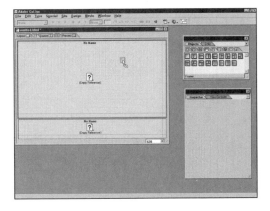

2.

The source code shows that inserting a new frame actually creates a nested frame set.

```
<frameset rows="80,*">
<frameset cols="*,*">
<frame src="(Empty Reference!)" name="No Name"
  noresize>
<frame src="(Empty Reference!)" name="No Name"
  noresize>
</frameset>
<frame src="(Empty Reference!)" name="No Name"
  noresize>
</frameset>
```

Changing the Frame Set Orientation

If the original frame set has a vertical orientation, the inserted frame will have a horizontal orientation, and vice versa.

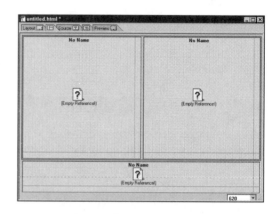

1.

To change the orientation of the nested frame set, first click on its border to select it.

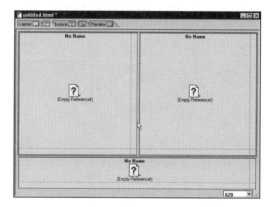

2.

In the Frame Set Inspector, click on the unselected Orientation radio button.

"Horizontal" and "Vertical" can be a bit confusing. Horizontally oriented frame sets have vertical borders, and vice versa.

3.

The reoriented frames are now in line with the original frame set's orientation.

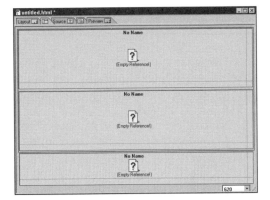

Deleting Frames and Frame Sets

If you want to modify one of GoLive's default frame sets—or if you simply change your mind about one of your own designs—it's even easier to delete frames than it is to add them.

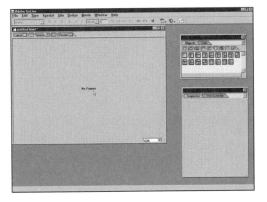

Deleting an Individual Frame

To delete an individual frame, click within it and then press your Del key.

Any other frame or frames in the same frame set will expand to take up the space left by the deleted frame.

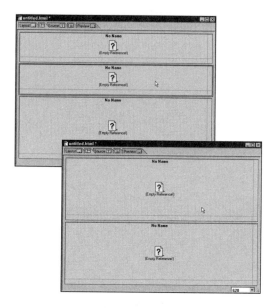

Deleting a Frame Set

To delete a frame set, first click on its border, and then press your Del key.

All frames in the deleted frame set disappear, leaving only the containing frame set.

If the frame set you delete contains nested frame sets, the nested frame sets also will be deleted.

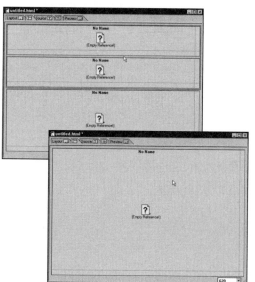

Modifying Frames

After a frame set, nested or otherwise, is in place, you may want to change a few of the details. We'll show you how to move frames and borders, set scrollbars, and decide whether your site's visitors have the right to change things around to suit themselves.

Moving Frames and Borders

In GoLive, the location of a border can be changed interactively. Even the location of a frame can be changed, although you cannot move a frame from one frame set into another.

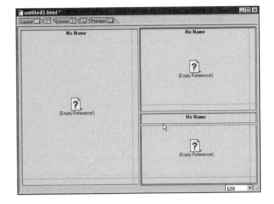

Moving a Frame

To move a frame from one place to another, click within it and drag it. An outline of the frame will accompany the mouse pointer as you move it.

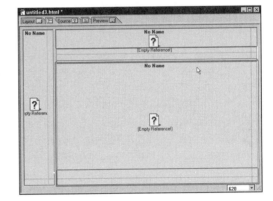

1.

The instant the mouse pointer enters the next frame, that frame will turn dark green.

Be careful when positioning the mouse pointer. If you are moving a large frame like this and the pointer is too far down to enter the other frame, the operation will fail.

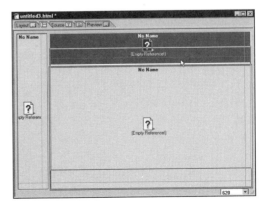

2.

As soon as the other frame turns dark green, you can release the mouse button. The two frames will change places with one another.

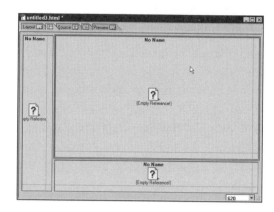

Moving an Entire Frame Set

Although a frame can't be moved outside the borders of its frame set, the entire frame set can be moved. Ctrl+click (Command+click on Macs) on the frame set border, and then drag and drop the frame set just as you would a frame.

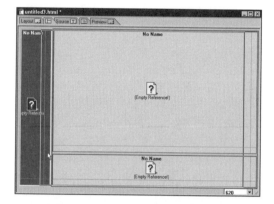

Moving a Border

To move a border, simply click on it and drag it from its current location to a new one.

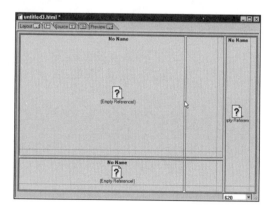

Using the Reset Size Option
to Move a Border

If a border won't move, you need to reset the Size option from Scale to either Percent or Pixel in either the Frame Inspector or the Frame Set Inspector.

The Frame Inspector is used if the border is between two frames in the same frame set. The Frame Set Inspector is used if the border is between two frame sets.

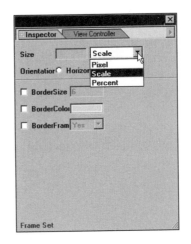

Resizing and Scrolling

Scrollbars automatically appear only when they are needed, unless you specifically override that setting. Likewise, site visitors will be able to resize frames unless you specify otherwise.

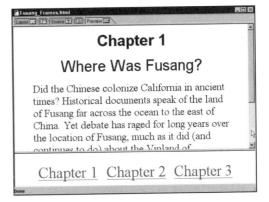

1.

Each frame has an indicator that shows the status of its scrollbar settings—a set of lines showing where the scrollbars will be. In the first frame, scrollbars are expressly disabled (no lines). In the second, they are expressly enabled (dark lines). In the third, they are set to automatic (light lines).

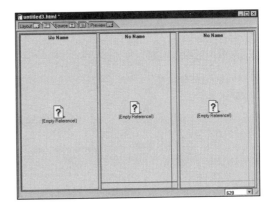

2.

To get to the scrollbar and resizing settings for a particular frame, click within that frame.

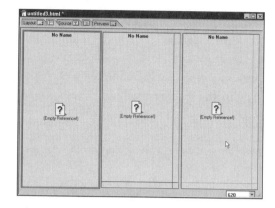

3.

In the Frame Inspector, click on the Scrolling drop-down list. Choose No to disable scrollbars, Yes to enable them, and Auto to let the user's Web browser decide if they are needed.

It's usually best to leave the setting at the default Auto.

4.

To allow the site's visitors to have the power to resize the frame by dragging the border in their Web browsers, click on the Resize Frame checkbox.

This has nothing to do with the Size options for use in GoLive. This affects only the site visitor, not the GoLive user.

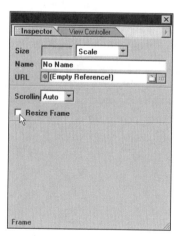

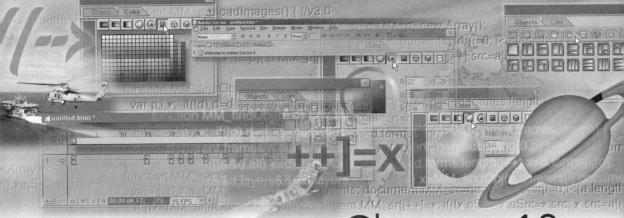

Chapter 10
Taking Control with Style Sheets

- Use CSS selectors to specify which elements are to be altered

- Set properties for fonts, borders, margins, background colors, and more

- Create and link external style sheets to easily format entire Web sites

Creating Styles

Cascading style sheets (CSS) are called that because of the way in which conflicts between the various types of styles are handled. For example, if an external style sheet defines H1 elements as blue and an embedded style sheet defines them as red, they end up as red. The authority cascades down from one level to the next. Styles are assigned by *selectors*, which are the handles that Web browsers use to understand how wide ranging a style is. We'll cover embedded style sheets first.

Setting Class Selectors

Classes are the most versatile kind of style selector. Because a class is both created and assigned by you, you can break out of the constraints of HTML.

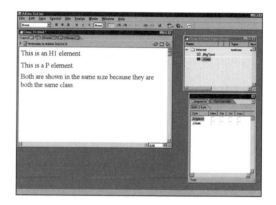

1.

If the Style Sheet window isn't already open, click on the Open CSS Interface button.

2.

Click on the New Class Selector button in the GoLive toolbar.

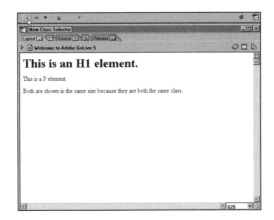

3.

In the CSS Selector Inspector, highlight the default class name and type your own over it. Class names should clearly describe what the style does, such as "reditalic" or "arialheading."

All class names begin with a dot (.), but you normally do not need to add it—GoLive usually does that automatically.

4.

The Style Sheet window will reflect the name change you have just made. Press Ctrl+S to save the changes (Mac users use Command+S).

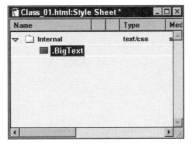

5.

After the class properties are defined (see "Setting Style Properties"), select the text you want to apply the style to, and then click on the Style tab in the Text Inspector. Click in the Inline checkbox to style only the highlighted text, the Par checkbox to style the entire paragraph, the Div checkbox to wrap the affected text in a DIV element (which does nothing but contain the selection), or the Area checkbox to style the whole page.

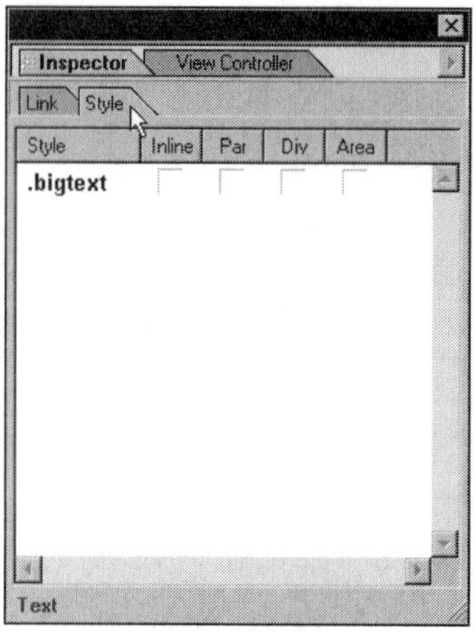

Setting Element Selectors

Element selectors are tremendously powerful and at the same time terribly limited. They change every single instance of a particular element such as all H1 headers or all I (italic) elements. If this is what you want, they're just what you need.

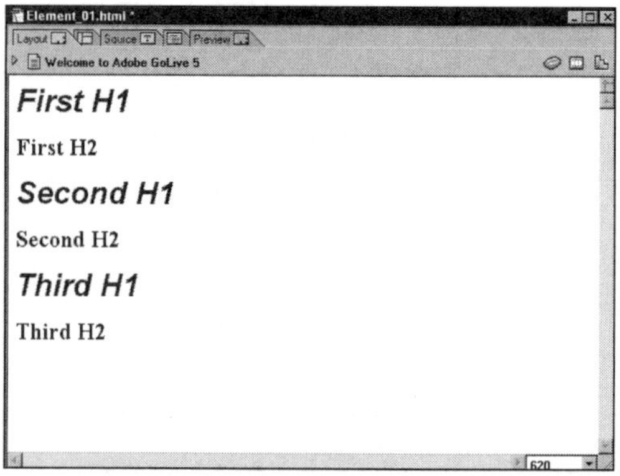

1.

If the Style Sheet window isn't already open, click on the Open CSS Interface button.

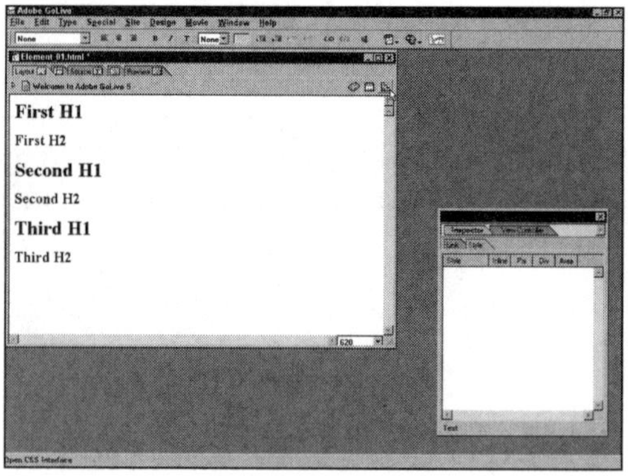

2.

Click on the New Element Selector button in the toolbar.

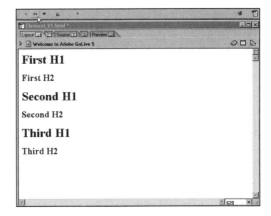

3.

In the CSS Selector Inspector, highlight the default name "element" and type the element you want to style over it. If you want to change all P elements, for example, type "P"; or change all H1 elements by typing "H1".

You also can add contextual selections, such as making every character within an H2 element italic by typing "H2 I".

4.

The Style Sheet window will reflect the name change you have just made. Press Ctrl+S to save the changes (Mac users use Command+S). As you define the class properties (see "Setting Style Properties"), all the affected elements change automatically.

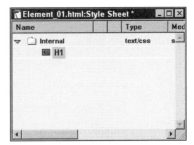

Setting ID Selectors

ID selectors have limited utility because they can be applied only to an individual element. Because that element can already be set to most styles in other ways, the only reason to use an ID selector is that the GoLive interface makes this the easiest way to set some unusual styles.

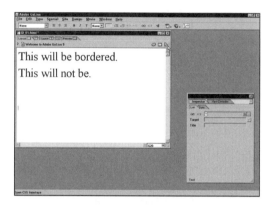

1.

If the Style Sheet window isn't already open, click on the Open CSS Interface button.

2.

Click on the New ID Selector button in the toolbar.

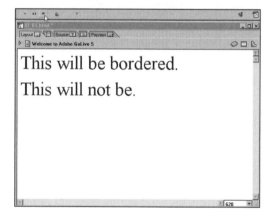

3.

In the CSS Selector Inspector, highlight the default ID name (#id) and type your own over it.

All ID names begin with a hash mark (#), and you need to leave it in—GoLive will not add it for you automatically if you type over it.

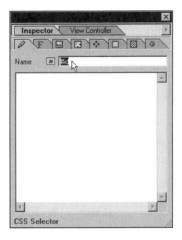

4.

After the class properties are defined (see "Setting Style Properties"), click on the Source tab to open the HTML Source Editor.

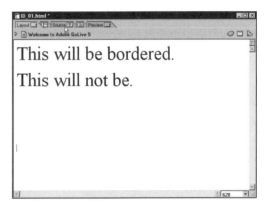

5.

In the HTML source code, add an ID attribute to the element you want to style. The value of the attribute must be the name of the ID style you created (not including the hash mark).

```
<html>

<head>
<meta http-equiv=□content-type□
 content=□text/html;charset=iso-8859-1">
<meta name=□generator□ content=□Adobe
 GoLive 5">
<title>Welcome to Adobe GoLive 5</title>
<style media=□screen□ type=□text/css□><!□
#Wrapped { border: solid thick }
□></style>
</head>

<body bgcolor=□#ffffff□>
<p><font size=□7" id=□Wrapped□>This will be
 bordered.</font></p>
<p><font size=□7">This will not be.</font></p>
</body>

</html>
```

Setting Style Properties

After a particular style selector has been created, it's time to set the properties it will cause a Web browser to show. GoLive has seven property tabs in its CSS Selector Inspector for you to work with.

Setting Font Properties

The Font Properties tab of the CSS Selector allows you to set color, size, line height, font family, style, weight, and decoration.

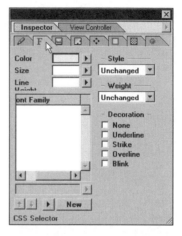

Selecting Color

To set one of the 16 common named colors, click on the Color arrow and select a name from the list. To use GoLive's color utilities, double-click on the Color box instead.

See Chapter 2 for more information on setting color in GoLive.

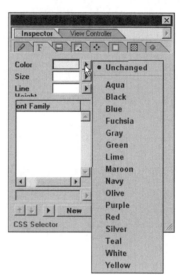

Changing Font Height

To set the height of the font, click on the Size arrow, and then choose a measurement method from the list. After you have chosen to use points (each point is 1/72 of an inch), pixels, inches, or whatever, there will be a default value in the Size box. Change the value to the one you want, taking care not to type over the measurement method.

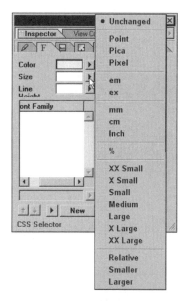

Adjusting Line Height

The height of the line is different from the height of the font. The line includes the white space that always lies between two sentences and that can be thought of as the distance between the bottom of one sentence and the bottom of the one above or below it. Click on the Line Height arrow, select a measurement method from the list, and then type your own value over the default value.

Selecting the Font Family

To select a font family, first click on the arrow below the Font Family box to bring up the font family listings.

Select a font family from the list.

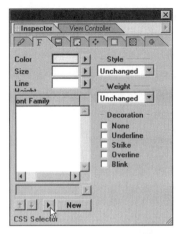

Changing the Order of Fonts

To change the order of the fonts in the listing, select the one you want to move, and then click on the up or down arrow buttons.

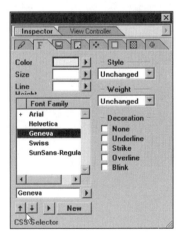

Adding Unlisted Fonts

To add an unlisted font, click on the New button, and then highlight the word "FontName" above the button and type the name of the unlisted font over it.

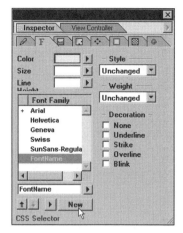

Changing the Font Style

To set a font style, click on the Style arrow and choose one of the styles from the drop-down list.

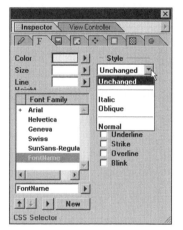

Changing the Font Weight

To set the font weight (essentially how thick or thin the lettering appears), click on the Weight arrow and select a setting from the drop-down list.

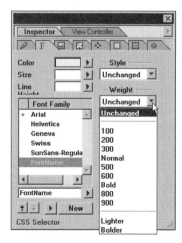

Choosing the Font Decoration

To choose a decorative style, click on one or more of the checkboxes under the word Decoration.

The Blink option, which causes text to blink on and off, is detested by the majority of Web designers, and works only in Netscape.

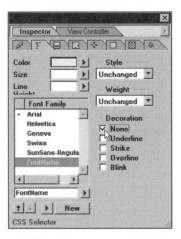

Setting Text Properties

The Text Properties tab of the CSS Selector allows you to set characteristics for indentation, word and letter spacing, vertical alignment, small capitals (Font Variant), capitalization (Transformation), and horizontal alignment.

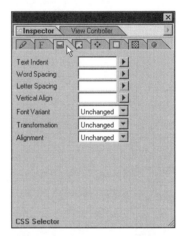

Selecting Indentation

To set indentation from the margin, click on the Text Indent arrow to bring up a list of measurement methods.

Select a measurement method from the list. A default value will show up in the Text Indent box. Type the desired value over the default value, taking care not to type over the measurement method.

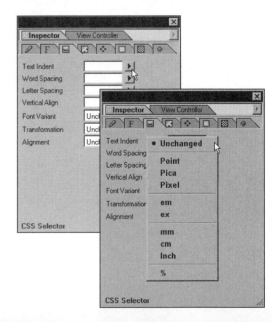

Changing Word and Letter Spacing

To increase the spacing between words or letters, click on the Word Spacing arrow or the Letter Spacing arrow and choose a measurement method from the list. A default value will show up in the Word Spacing or Letter Spacing box. Type the desired value over the default value, taking care not to type over the measurement method.

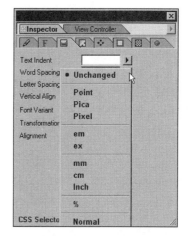

Setting the Vertical Alignment

To set vertical alignment, click on the Vertical Align arrow and choose an alignment method from the list.

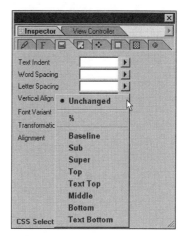

Setting Capitalization

To change all lettering to small capital letters, click on the Font Variant arrow and choose Small Caps from the list. Choose Normal to change all lettering back.

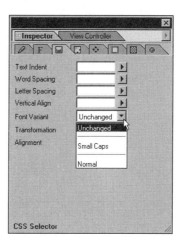

Setting Capitalization Rules

To set capitalization rules, click on the Transformation arrow and choose Capitalize to set all first letters of words as capitals, Uppercase to set all letters as capitals, Lowercase to set all letters to lower case, or None to undo any earlier settings.

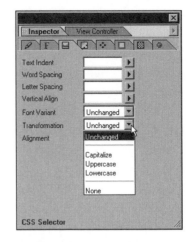

Setting the Horizontal Alignment

To set horizontal alignment, click on the Alignment arrow and choose an alignment method from the list.

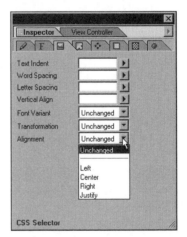

Setting Block Properties

The Block Properties tab of the CSS Selector allows you to control the amount of space between one block-level element and another, how much padding there is between an element and its outer edge, what the overall size of a block is, whether it can float free of its surroundings, and whether other floating elements can sit beside it.

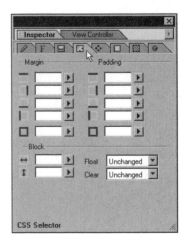

Block-level elements are those that automatically create a line break before the next element, such as P (paragraph), TABLE, DIV, and the like.

Margin, Padding, and Block Settings

Margin, Padding, and Block settings all work the same basic way. Click on one of the arrows and choose a measurement unit from an identical list, and then type your own value over the default one that shows in the text box, taking care not to type over the measurement method.

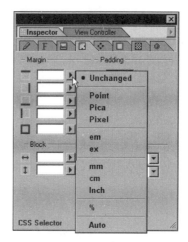

Margin Values

Margin values determine how far an element is from the edge of the Web page and the nearest other elements. Each text box/arrow combination shows a darkened outline to indicate which margin it sets. The bottom one, with all four sides dark, sets all four margins at once.

Padding Values

Padding values determine how far the contents of a styled block-level element are indented from the edges of its own block, just as cell padding works in tables.

See Chapter 8 for information on cell padding in tables.

Block Values

Block values determine the size of the block-level element. The first setting is for horizontal size, and the second is for vertical size.

Setting Block Alignment

Click on the Float arrow to choose left or right alignment values that work just like those of image elements. Left drops the element to the left margin below its current position and lets text flow to its right; Right drops the element to the right margin and lets text flow to its left. None removes all previous settings.

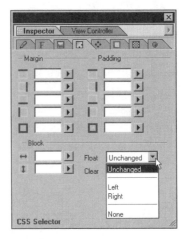

Working with Floating Elements

Click on the Clear arrow to choose whether a floating element is allowed to coexist with other floating elements. Left drops the element below another floating element on its left, Right drops it below another one on its right, and Both leaves all floating elements alone.

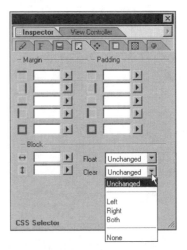

Setting Position Properties

Click on the Position tab to access the position properties. The element positioning possibilities are perhaps the most important of all the CSS property settings. Especially important to those who come to the Web from a traditional print background, absolute positioning gives unprecedented power to control the appearance of Web pages.

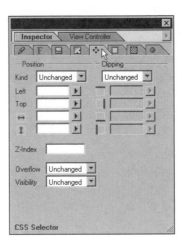

1.

Click on the Kind arrow to select the type of positioning this style will use. Absolute is based on the top left corner of the Web page, Static is normal HTML positioning, and Relative is based on the preceding element on the page.

2.

To set the location of the left side of the element, click on the Left arrow and choose a measurement method. A default value will show up in the Left box. Type the desired value over the default value, taking care not to type over the measurement method. Top works the same way, but sets the location of the top of the element.

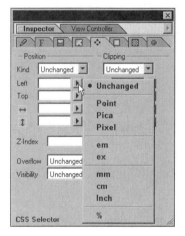

3.

To set the width of the element, click on the Width arrow and select a measurement type. A default value will show up in the Width box. Type the desired value over the default value, taking care not to type over the measurement method. The Height setting works the same way, using the same list.

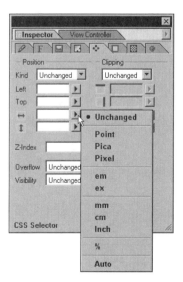

Overlapping Elements

Enter a Z-Index value to determine which element is on top of other ones that overlap it. The lower the value, the farther back an element is; the higher the value, the farther forward it is. In other words, the element with the highest Z-Index value is on top of all other elements; the element with the lowest Z-Index value is beneath all other elements.

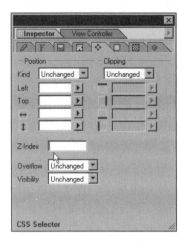

Handling Oversized Elements

Click on the Overflow arrow to set what happens if the element the style is applied to is larger than the specified size. Visible makes it all show regardless, Scroll sets up scrollbars at the edges of the element, and Hidden cuts off the overflowing portion. Auto leaves everything up to the browser the page is viewed in.

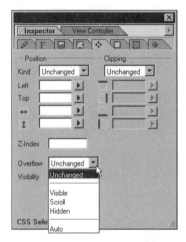

Determining Visibility

Click on the Visibility arrow to set whether an element with this style is visible. The Visible and Hidden options are obvious. Inherited means that the visibility of the element that contains this element automatically sets the value.

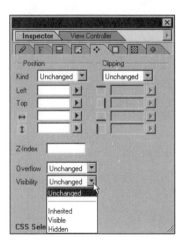

Clipping an Element's Content

To clip the content of an element, click on the Clipping arrow and choose a clipping method from the drop-down list. Choose Auto to leave it up to the Web browser, Inherit to use the clipping method of the parent element, or Rect to specify a rectangular area.

Clipping can be used to hide part of an element, such as the answer to a quiz question.

Using the Rect Option

For the Rect option, click on the arrow for each side of the rectangle and select a measurement method. A default value will show up in each side's box. Type the desired value over the default value, taking care not to type over the measurement method.

Setting Border Properties

The Border Properties tab lets you define the color and characteristics of a border around the element this style is applied to. You can either set a full border or limit the border to one or more sides.

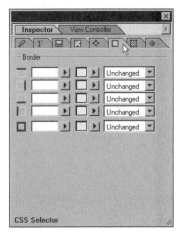

1.

Click on the arrow next to one of the sides of the rectangle or on the full rectangle and choose a measurement method from the list. A default value will show up in the text box. Type the desired value over the default value, taking care not to type over the measurement method.

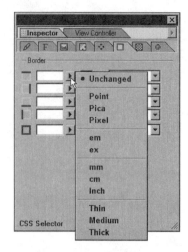

2.

Click on the arrow next to the color box for the selected side and choose a named color from the list. To use GoLive's color utilities, double-click on the Color box instead.

See Chapter 2 for more information on setting color in GoLive.

3.

Click on the arrow on the right side to choose a line style for the border from the drop-down list.

If you choose each side individually instead of all four at once, you can set different border styles for each side.

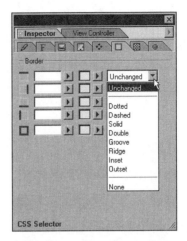

Setting Background Properties

The Background Properties tab of the CSS Selector Inspector is where you set background images and colors for any element this style is applied to.

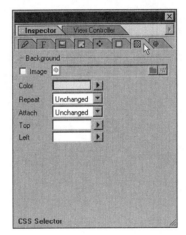

Adding a Background Image

To add a background image to anything styled with this selector, click on the Image checkbox. Specify an image file by using the Point and Shoot button, by typing in the file name, or by using the Browse button.

See Chapter 5 for details on specifying image files.

Setting Background Color

To set a background color, click on the Color arrow and select a name from the list. To use GoLive's color utilities, double-click on the Color box instead.

See Chapter 2 for more information on setting color in GoLive.

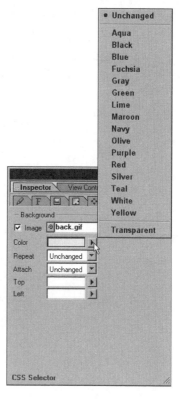

Setting the Background Image's Tiling Routine

To set the background image's tiling routine, click on the Repeat arrow and choose an option from the drop-down list. Repeat is normal tiling, Repeat x is horizontal tiling only, and Repeat y is vertical tiling only; Once means no tiling at all.

Setting the Background Image's Scrolling Properties

To set the background image's scrolling properties, click on the Attach arrow and choose an option from the drop-down list. Scroll means it scrolls, and Fixed means it doesn't.

Positioning Background Images

Finally, to position the background image relative to the element, click on the Top and Left arrows and choose a measurement method from the list. Default values will show up in the text boxes. Type the desired values over the default values, taking care not to type over the measurement method.

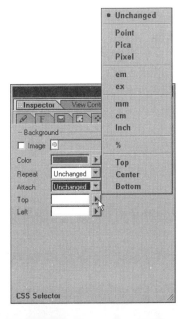

Setting List Properties

CSS helps you customize the properties of both ordered and unordered lists, including the ability to use custom images instead of the default HTML bullets.

See Chapter 4 for more information on lists.

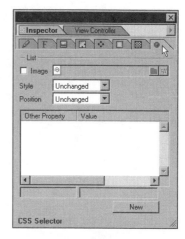

Using Custom Images for Lists

To use a custom image of your own (like a star or colored bullet), click on the Image checkbox. Specify an image file by using the Point and Shoot button, by typing in the file name, or by using the Browse button.

See Chapter 5 for details on specifying image files.

Selecting Bullets or Numbering Systems

To choose the kind of bullets or numbering system the list uses, click on the Style arrow and choose an option from the drop-down list.

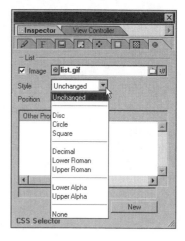

Indenting List Items

To choose whether the list items are indented, click on the Position arrow and choose an option from the drop-down list. (Outside is indented.)

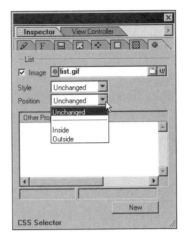

Using External Style Sheets

Although an embedded style sheet affects only the Web page it's a part of, external style sheets are separate files that can control many pages at once. They also have the advantage of being reusable—once you create an external style sheet, you can apply it at will to any page, regardless of whether it's on the original Web site.

Creating External Style Sheets

External style sheets are mainly used to set a common appearance among all the pages of a Web site.

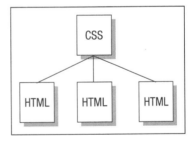

1.

Choose File|New Special|Style Sheet Document from the menu.

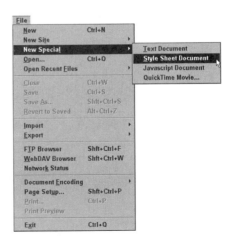

2.

The Style Sheet window opens, just as when you're creating an embedded style sheet; but, instead of the name of an HTML file and the notation that it's a style sheet, it has a distinct file name ending in .css.

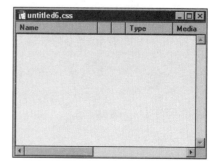

3.

Selector types are added from the toolbar, just as with an embedded style sheet, and the processes with the CSS Selector Inspector are identical. The only difference is that the style sheet is saved as a unique external file.

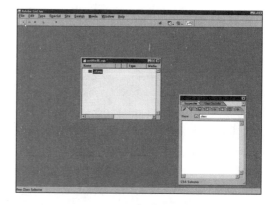

4.

Embedded style sheets also can be converted into external style sheets. Simply right-click in the Style Sheet window for an embedded style sheet and select Export Internal CSS from the pop-up menu, and then save the file.

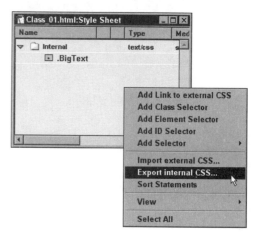

Chapter 11
Getting Dynamic
with DHTML

- Add interactivity with JavaScript

- Use actions to set and read cookies

- Animate floating boxes

Dynamic Web Pages

GoLive has lots of ways to add a bit of sizzle and pop to your Web pages, from JavaScript actions to animation paths. Some of these methods are used to add interactivity to your pages, while others work independently of what your site's visitors do.

Adding JavaScript Actions

GoLive's built-in JavaScript actions are organized into several different categories. The actions must be keyed either to a Head Action or a Body Action object or to a link.

Attaching JavaScript Actions

The objects for attaching JavaScript actions to the Head or Body of a Web page are found on the Smart tab of the Objects palette.

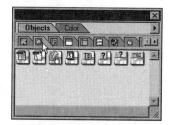

Setting Actions in the Web Page Head

To set a JavaScript action in the Head, you use the Head Action icon.

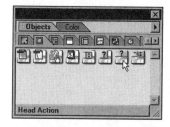

1.

If the Head section of your Web page isn't open, click on the Toggle Head Section button.

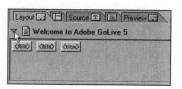

2.

Drag the Head Action icon into the Head section and drop it there.

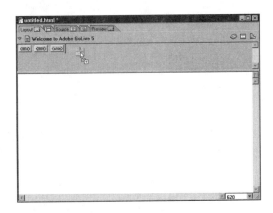

You can combine Steps 3 and 4 by dragging the Head Action icon onto the Toggle Head Section button, waiting a moment for the Head section to open, and then dropping the Head Action icon into the Head section.

3.

Make sure the icon in the Head section is selected. In the Action Inspector, select a trigger from the Exec. drop-down menu. OnLoad triggers when the page loads, OnUnload triggers when the visitor leaves the page, and OnParse triggers when the action is reached during the parsing process. OnCall is used only to trigger the action from a Call Action.

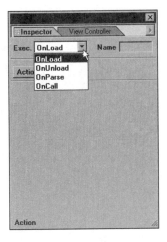

See "The Specials Actions," later in this chapter, for information on Call Action.

4.

Click on the Action button to access the JavaScript actions menu, and then select the desired action.

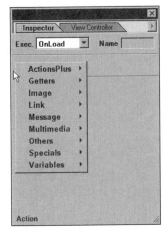

Setting Actions in the Web Page Body

To set a JavaScript action in the Body, use the Body Action icon.

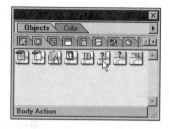

1.

Drag the Body Action icon into the Body section and drop it there.

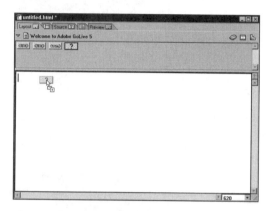

2.

Click on the Action button to access the JavaScript actions menu, and then select the desired action.

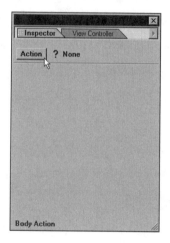

Linking with a JavaScript Action

To set a JavaScript action for a link, you select the link. If you want only the action and no real link, type a hash mark (#) as the link in the Text Inspector or Image Inspector.

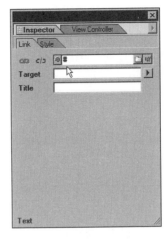

1.

In the Actions palette, select a trigger from the Events listing (Mouse Click, for example, if you want the action to take place when the link is clicked on). Use the scroll bars, if necessary, to view all the possible selections.

If the Actions palette isn't open, choose Window|Actions from the menu.

2.

Click on the Add Action button. This creates a blank action called "None" and activates the Action button.

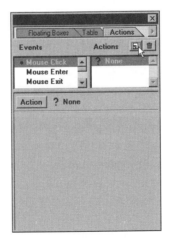

Events—the occurrences that trigger actions—can have multiple actions assigned to them. To add more actions, click on the Add Action button again. To delete an action, select it and click on the Trashcan button.

3.

Click on the Action button to access the JavaScript actions menu, and then select the desired action for the link.

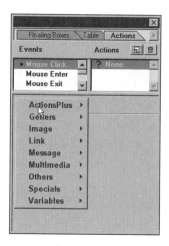

Exploring GoLive's Actions

GoLive's actions—built-in JavaScripts that you can just drop into place—give you a great deal of power without the bother of learning programming. Just set a few options, and your pages are as good as anything out there.

The ActionsPlus Actions

Choosing the ActionsPlus option gets you a potpourri of JavaScript actions ranging from cookie deletion to slide shows.

The ConfirmLink Action

The ConfirmLink action generates a pop-up message asking users who have just clicked on a link if they really want to go to the linked page. Enter the message you want displayed in the popup in the Message text box, and then enter the URL and, if desired, the name of a target frame.

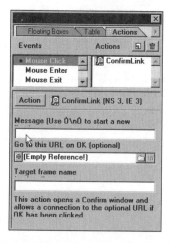

The DailyImageURL Action

The DailyImageURL action displays a different image, depending on what day it is. The base image must have a name, which is chosen from the drop-down list. The replacement images, which all must be the same size as the base image, are selected normally.

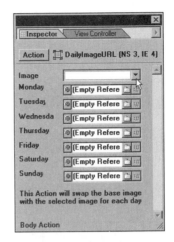

See Chapter 5 for more information on image selection.

The DailyRedirect Action

The DailyRedirect action sends a visitor to a different Web page, depending upon which day it is. Set each day's page by using the Point and Shoot button, by typing the URL, or by using the Browse button.

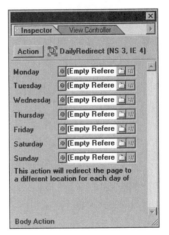

See Chapter 6 for information on setting Web page links.

The DeleteCookie Action

The DeleteCookie action is used to delete the cookie whose name is specified in the Cookie text box.

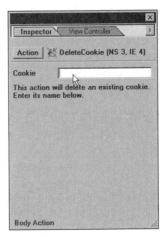

The ForceFrame Action

The ForceFrame action keeps a framed page together with its frame set, no matter how it is linked to. Specify the name of the frame set in the Frameset box by using the Point and Shoot button, by typing, or by using the Browse button. Type the name of the frame in which the page should be displayed in the Frame text box.

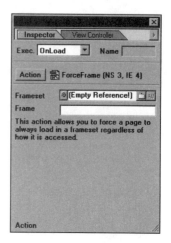

The KillFrame Action

The KillFrame action will keep a page from being displayed in a frame set. There are no variables to set.

This action protects your pages from being used as a part of someone else's framed site.

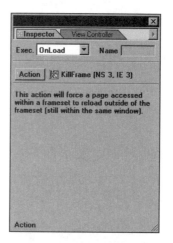

The Password Action

To use the Password action to password-protect a page, you first load the makepassword.html file into your browser and click on its link. In a typical Windows installation, this file is located at C:\Program Files\Adobe\GoLive 5.0_ENG\Modules\JScripts\Actions\ActionsPlus\.

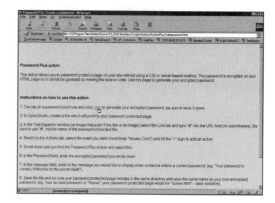

1.

Enter a password into the text box in the pop-up window, and then click on OK.

2.

Write down both the plain and encrypted versions of the password, and then click on OK.

3.

Set up a link with only a hash mark (#) as the URL. In the Actions palette, type the encrypted password into the first text box and enter a pop-up message in the second text box. Use the unencrypted password as the name of the page you want protected, and put both it and the page that has the link in the same folder.

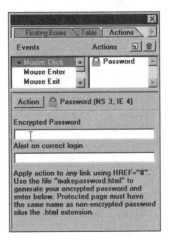

The SlideShow Action

To use the SlideShow action to create an interactive slide show, create a series of images named 01.gif, 02.gif, and so forth. (They also can be JPEG files, but you cannot mix the file types.) Give 01.gif a name and select that name by clicking on the Base Image drop-down list. Enter the number of image files in the slide show in the Number of text box. Select a checkbox to set the method of playback.

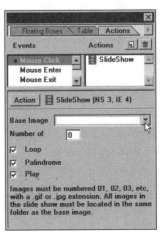

The SlideShowAuto Action

To use the SlideShowAuto action to create an automated slide show, create a series of images named 01.gif, 02.gif, and so forth. (They also can be JPEG files, but you cannot mix the file types.) Give 01.gif a name and select that name by clicking on the Base Image drop-down list. Enter the number of image files in the slide show in the # of images text box. Enter the delay in seconds between images in the Interval text box. Select the Stop at end of slideshow checkbox to prevent looping.

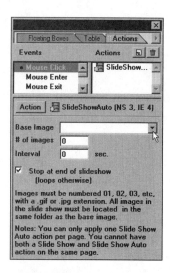

The SlideShowAutoStop Action

If you chose not to prevent looping, the only way to stop an automated slide show is via the SlideShowAutoStop action. There are no variables to set.

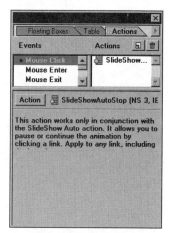

The Target2Frames Action

The Target2Frames action lets a single link load two frames at once. This lets you change the Web pages that load into two different frames instead of just one, as with a normal link. Enter the name of one frame in the Frame 1 text box, and then set the page to be loaded into it in the Link box. Repeat for the second frame using the Frame 2 boxes.

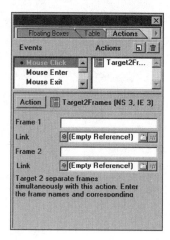

The TargetRemote Action

Create a page that has a series of links. Add a TargetRemote action to each link, specifying the URL of the page you want to display. Open the file in a browser window created by the Open Window action.

See "The Link Actions" for information on using the Open Window action.

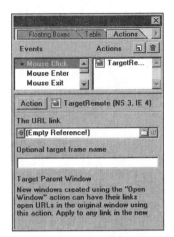

The TimeRedirect Action

The TimeRedirect action is used to load a different page depending upon the hour. Set the hour of the day you want to use in the Time text box. Deselect the PM checkbox to set the time for AM. Set the URL of Web pages in either or both of the Before and At/after boxes.

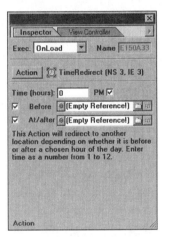

The VisitorCookie Action

The VisitorCookie action uses a cookie to redirect visitors to a new Web page if this is not their first visit. Enter a name for the cookie in the text box. Set the URL for the page you want veteran visitors to go to.

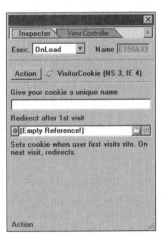

The Getters Actions

"Getters" are used to get values—either the position of a floating box or the contents of a form field.

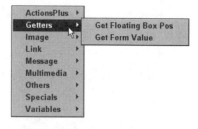

The Get Floating Box Pos

The Get Floating Box Pos is used to get the current position of a floating box—a "layer" in normal HTML terms. Click on the arrow to select a floating box from the drop-down list.

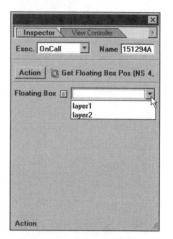

The Get Form Value

The Get Form Value is used to read the current contents of a text field. Type the name of the form that contains the text field in the Form text box. Type the name of the text field in the Element text box.

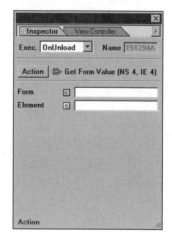

The Image Actions

The three Image actions allow you to preload images so that they are available without further download time, to set up random image changes, and to swap images.

The Preload Image Action

The Preload Image action makes sure that an image is loaded before the Web page is displayed. Use the Point and Shoot button, type the URL of the image, or use the Browse button.

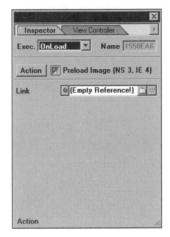

The RandomImage Action

The RandomImage action will replace the base image with one of up to three other images. As the name implies, the sequence in which the other three images are displayed is random. Choose the name of the base image from the drop-down list, and then specify the URLs of the other images.

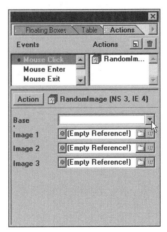

The Set Image URL Action

The Set Image URL action changes which image is displayed by changing the URL of an image. Click on the arrow and choose the name of the first image from the Image drop-down list, and then set the URL of the second image in the Link box.

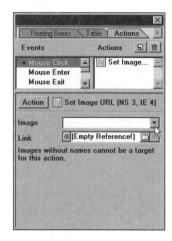

The Link Actions

The four Link actions give you various ways to take over a visitor's Web browser.

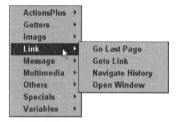

The Go Last Page Action

The Go Last Page action is used to force the browser to retrace one step just as if visitors had clicked the Back button in their browsers.

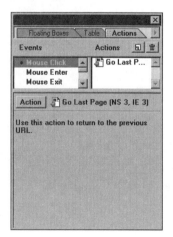

The Goto Link Action

The Goto Link action works just as a normal link does. Specify the URL of the linked file in the Link box. Optionally, specify a target frame in the Target text box.

The Navigate History Action

The Navigate History action makes the Web browser jump a specific distance forward or backward in the browser's own history listing. Specify the size of the jump by entering a number in the Go Where text box. Negative numbers take the browser back in the history.

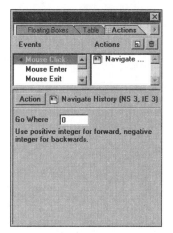

The Open Window Action

The Open Window action launches a second instance of the visitor's Web browser. Set the URL of the page to be displayed in the Link box. If desired, specify the window width and height in the Size text boxes.

The second browser window is fully functional by default. To disable any features, deselect the appropriate checkboxes.

The Message Actions

The three Message actions are used to add HTML to an existing Web page, to launch a pop-up message window, and to create a message in the browser's status bar.

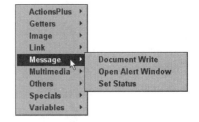

Using Document Write

To write new HTML code within an existing Web page, place a Body Action icon in the Web page (see "Setting Actions in the Web Page Body" earlier in this chapter). In the Body Action Inspector, enter the text you want displayed within the Web page in the HTML text box.

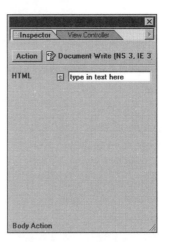

Key the Open Alert Window

The Open Alert Window action is used to send a message to a visitor. You can key it to practically any kind of trigger, such as opening a new page or clicking on a link. In the Inspector, enter the text you want displayed in the pop-up alert window.

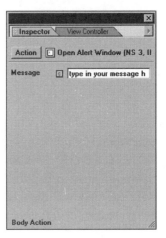

The Set Status Action

The Set Status action is used to set up a scrolling message in the status bars of visitors' Web browsers. Enter the message in the Status text box.

Think twice before using this action because the message takes over the status bar where people are accustomed to seeing other information. It can be very annoying to visitors if the usual information is overwritten unnecessarily.

The Multimedia Actions

There are 11 different multimedia actions. They deal with controlling floating boxes and timeline animations.

The Drag Floating Box Action

The Drag Floating Box action makes a floating box capable of being dragged around the screen of a Web browser and dropped in a new location. It should be set via a Head Action item. Leave Exec. set at OnLoad, and then click on the arrow to choose a floating box from the drop-down list.

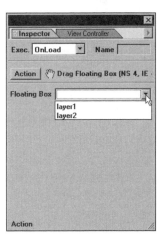

The Flip Move Action

The Flip Move action moves a floating box back and forth between two specific locations. Choose the floating box from the drop-down list. Enter the left and top coordinates of the starting point in the Position 1 text boxes. Enter the coordinates for the end point in the Position 2 text boxes. Make sure the Animation box is checked so that the floating box doesn't just jump from one position to the next. Enter the speed in the Ticks text box (a tick is 1/60 of a second).

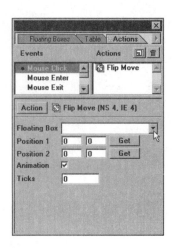

The Get button will automatically get the current position of a floating box.

The Move By Action

The Move By action moves a floating box a certain number of pixels horizontally, vertically, or both at once when the action is triggered. Choose the floating box from the drop-down list. Enter the horizontal distance in pixels in the DeltaX text box and the vertical distance in the DeltaY text box.

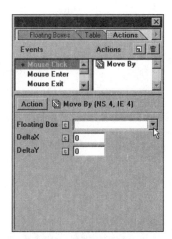

The Move To Action

The Move To action moves a floating box from any location to a specific new location. Choose the floating box from the drop-down list. Enter the left and top coordinates of the new location in the Position text boxes. Type the speed of movement in the Ticks text box (a tick is 1/60 of a second).

The Get button will automatically get the current position of a floating box.

Playing a Scene

The Play Scene action launches a timeline animation scene. Click on the arrow to select an existing scene from the drop-down list.

See "Using Animation Timelines" later in this chapter.

Playing an Audio File

The Play Sound action activates an audio file. Choose the name of the audio file from the drop-down list.

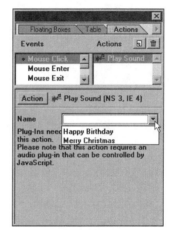

Hiding or Showing a Floating Box

The ShowHide action causes a floating box to become either visible or invisible. Choose the floating box from the first drop-down menu. Choose the visibility setting from the Mode drop-down list. Hide and Show are obvious, and Toggle means to change from whatever the current visibility setting is to its opposite.

The Stop Complete Action

The Stop Complete action instantly halts the execution of any timeline animations that are taking place. There are no options to set.

The Stop Scene Action

The Stop Scene action is used to halt the execution of a particular timeline animation scene. Choose the scene from the drop-down list.

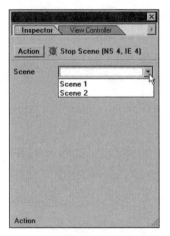

The Stop Sound Action

The Stop Sound action halts the playing of a particular audio file. Choose the name of the file from the drop-down list.

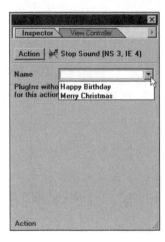

Creating Fade Effects

The Wipe Transition action causes a floating box to appear to fade in or out. Choose the floating box from the first drop-down list. Choose the transition method from the Transition drop-down list. Type in a value for the number of steps for the transition to take.

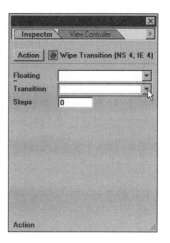

Lower numbers make for faster, but clumsier, transitions.

The Others Actions

The Others actions are another potpourri: a Netscape fix, window resizing, scrolling, and setting background color.

Netscape Fix

The Netscape CSS Fix action solves a problem in which Netscape Navigator 4, when resized, loses layer information. It should be used with a Head Action item and executed OnLoad.

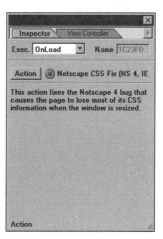

Resizing the Browser Window

The ResizeWindow action is used to change the width and/or height of the browser window. Enter a value in pixels in the Width and/or Height text boxes.

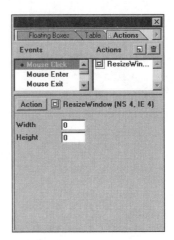

Scrolling Actions

The four scroll actions (Scroll Down, Scroll Left, Scroll Right, and Scroll Up) all work identically by moving a floating box in the specified direction. Enter the distance to be moved in the Scroll pixels text box and the speed of movement in the second text box.

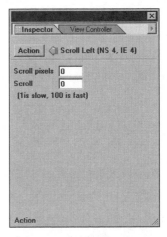

Setting Background Color

The Set BackColor action changes the background color of the Web page. Click within the Background color box to launch the Colors palette and choose a color.

See Chapter 2 for how to use the Colors palette.

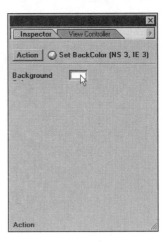

The Specials Actions

The Specials actions are composed of a few programming aids and some conditional testing. The Intersection, KeyCompare, and Timeout actions are grayed out at first.

Creating Sequential Actions

The Action Group action is used to create a set of actions that will be performed sequentially when a single trigger is activated. Click on the Add Action button, and then click on the lower Action button to specify which action to add and what properties it has. Repeat this process until you have added all the actions you need.

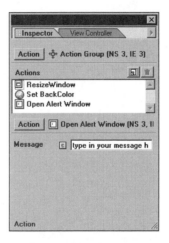

The Call Action Action

The Call Action action is used to launch any Head Action item whose method is set to OnCall. Choose the action to be called from the drop-down list. Only those actions fitting the requirements will be shown on it.

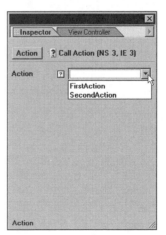

The Call Function Action

The Call Function action is used to launch a custom-written JavaScript function. Select the function from the Function drop-down list. Enter any arguments you wish to feed to the function in the Arguments text box.

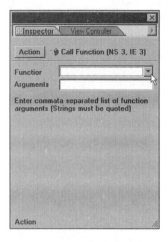

The Condition and Idle Actions

The Condition and Idle actions both test for the existence of a particular condition and react accordingly. The Condition action is a one-shot action while Idle can keep reacting after the first time. Click on the Action button and choose from Intersection, KeyCompare, or Timeout from the Specials actions.

To keep Idle running indefinitely, deselect the Exit Idle If Condition returns True checkbox.

The Intersection Action

The Intersection action tests for an overlap condition between two different floating boxes. Choose the two floating boxes from the drop-down lists.

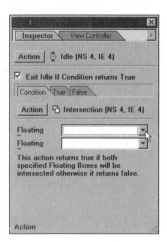

The KeyCompare Action

The KeyCompare action waits for a particular key to be pressed. Enter the ASCII code for the key in the CharCode text box.

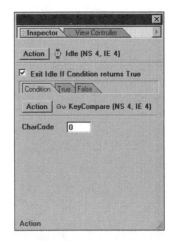

The Timeout Action

The Timeout action watches for a certain amount of time to elapse before taking an action. Enter the number of seconds to wait in the Timeout text box.

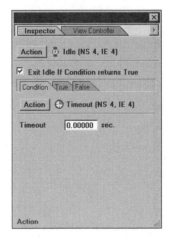

Conditional Actions

Click on the True and False tabs and set the actions to be taken when the conditions are and aren't true.

You do not set a False condition for the KeyCompare action.

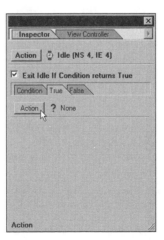

The Variables Actions

The Variables actions are concerned with managing variable values and using these values in cookies—data files written to your visitors' hard drives. The Test Variable option is grayed out at first.

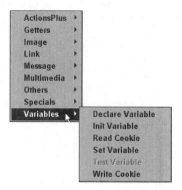

The Declare Variable Action

The Declare Variable action is used to create a variable. Enter a name for the variable in the Name text box. Specify the data type by choosing one from the Type drop-down list. If you want to write the variable and its value to a cookie, enter the name of the cookie in the Cookie text box.

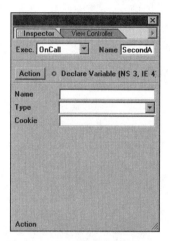

The Init Variable Action

The Init Variable action is used to set an initial value for a variable in a Head Action item. Choose the variable from the Variable drop-down list. The Value segment will vary depending upon the data type—it will become a standard link box for a URL variable, for instance.

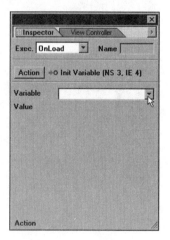

The Read Cookie Action

The Read Cookie action is used to gather information previously saved on a visitor's hard drive. Enter the name of the cookie you want to read in the Name text box.

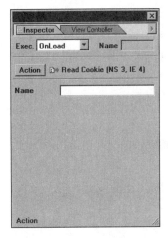

The Set Variable Action

The Set Variable action is identical to the Init Variable action in its function. Variable values are *initialized*—set to a particular starting value—when the page is loaded. The Set Variable action is designed to be called at some point after the page is loaded, usually in response to some user activity.

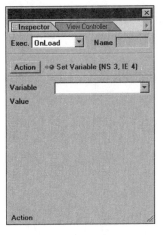

The Test Variable Action

The Test Variable action is available only as a subset of the Idle or Condition actions. Choose the variable from the Variable drop-down list. The Value options vary depending upon the data type. Choose an operation such as Equal or Less Than from the Operation drop-down list.

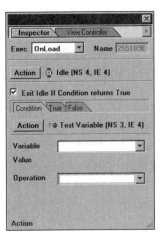

The Write Cookie Action

The Write Cookie action is used to record the values of variables on a visitor's hard drive. Type a name for the cookie in the Name text box. In the Expires text box, enter a time lapse after which the cookie is no longer valid. In the Domain and Path text boxes, if desired, enter a domain and path that must be matched. Select the Secure text box to prevent insecure transmission of the cookie.

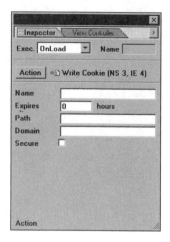

Using Animation Timelines

Animation timelines let you move floating boxes around on the screen. Because this also means that the contents of those floating boxes move with them, you have the capability to animate the entire contents of your Web page.

The Timeline Editor

The Timeline Editor is invoked by clicking on the button that looks like a filmstrip at the upper right side of the Layout Editor.

1.

The Timeline Editor shows one track for each floating box on the page. Initially, the first floating box is selected, but you can click on any of the tracks to select another one.

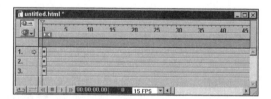

2.

There is, at first, one blue box for each floating box. These "keyframes" set the position of a floating box at a particular time. The time scale at the top of the Timeline Editor shows when this position is reached. Because this is the starting position, the time scale shows zero.

3.

New keyframes are added by Ctrl+clicking at various points along the timeline. The yellow play range indicator expands to show the full span of time covered.

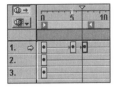

Mac users should use Command+click.

4.

Click on a keyframe and then, in the Layout Editor, drag the floating box to the position you want it to occupy at that time. Repeat for each keyframe. A line will show the animation path you are creating.

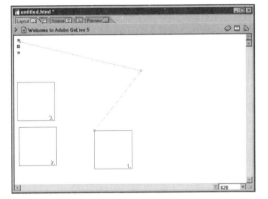

5.

To add actions to the animation, Ctrl+click in the Action Track. These actions do not need to have object triggers; their position in the timeline is the trigger.

Mac users should use Command+click.

Recording a Timeline

To quickly create a complex timeline without having to manually add all the keyframes, you can record the movement of a floating box as you drag it.

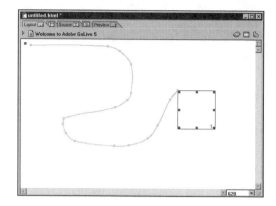

1.

In the Floating Box Inspector, click on the Record button.

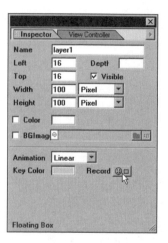

2.

Place the mouse cursor over one of the sides of the floating box and drag it around the screen along the pathway you want it to follow in the timeline animation. When you release the mouse button, the recording ceases.

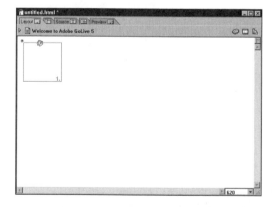

3.

Keyframes reflecting the movements you made are automatically created in the Timeline Editor.

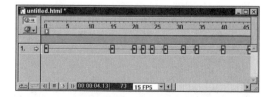

Part II
Projects

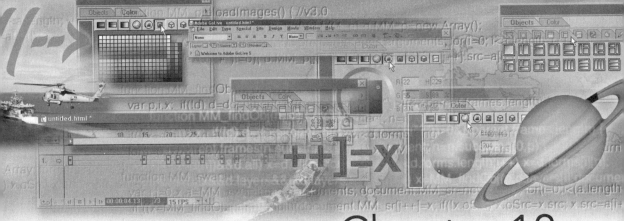

Chapter 12
Projects with Pages and Sites

Project 1: Make a page template

Project 2: Create a navigation bar component

Project 3: Modify source code

Going Beyond Basics

Web sites, of course, are what GoLive is all about, and Web pages are the building blocks of those sites. This chapter offers a few projects to help you get better acquainted with what you can do with both.

Project 1: Make a Page Template

The standard blank page that GoLive creates when you choose File|New from the menu may not be suitable for your particular needs. This project shows how to create your own New Page template and make GoLive use it instead of the default one.

1.

You can make any existing Web page into your default New Page in GoLive. In this project, we're using the standard blank "untitled.html" to start with.

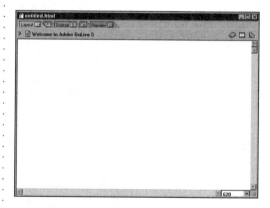

2.

Even though the standard default page is blank, a look at its source code shows that it actually contains several different settings—such as the page title and background color.

```
<html>
<head>
<meta http-equiv=□content-type□
 content=□text/html;charset=iso-8859-1">
<meta name=□generator□ content=□Adobe
 GoLive 5">
<title>Welcome to Adobe GoLive 5</title>
</head>
<body bgcolor=□#ffffff□>
<p></p>
</body>
</html>
```

3.

The first step is to change the page title from "Welcome to Adobe GoLive 5" to something more appropriate. Click on the Page icon in the top left corner of the Layout Editor.

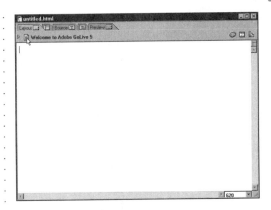

4.

In the Page Inspector, highlight the default title and type your own title over it. We'll be building a default page style to be used on all the pages for a fictitious Web design client, so we'll use the title "Pearson Project Template Page."

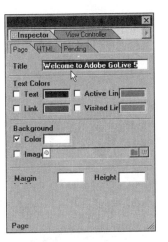

5.

Next, we'll be setting default colors for the page. Click on the Text checkbox so that it is selected, and then click on the color box next to it.

6.

Although you can use any color choosing method you wish, in this example, we'll be using named colors, so click on the Named Colors tab in the Color palette.

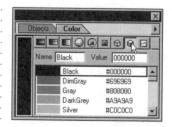

7.

Scroll down the list of colors until you come to White, and then click on it.

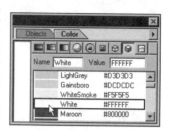

8.

Back in the Page Inspector, click on the Link checkbox so tha it is selected, and then click on the color box next to it.

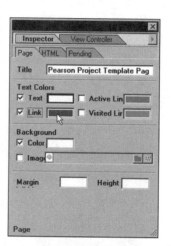

9.

Scroll down the list of colors until you come to DeepSkyBlue, and then click on it.

10.

Back in the Page Inspector, click on the Visited Link checkbox so that it is selected, and then click on the color box next to it.

We're not bothering to set the Active Link color, because it exists only during the moment a link is clicked on. The Link and Visited Link colors, however, are permanent parts of the page.

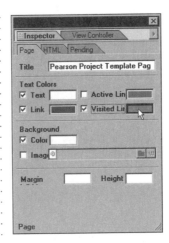

11.

Scroll up the list of colors until you come to Gold, and then click on it.

12.

GoLive has a default background color of white. For this template, we want black instead, and the text and link colors were chosen with that in mind. Because the Color checkbox is already selected by default, all you need to do is click on the color box next to it.

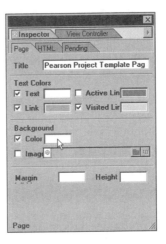

13.

Scroll to the top of the list and click on Black.

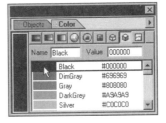

14.

Choose File|Save As from the menu and give the file the name "Pearson_Default.html".

If you need to create different default pages for different projects of your own, you may want to create a folder in which you store a copy of each.

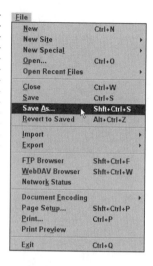

15.

Next, we'll be adding some common elements to the default page, starting with a company logo bracketed by two horizontal lines. Click on the Objects tab to open the Objects palette.

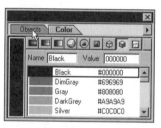

16.

Click on the Line icon, drag it into the Layout Editor, and drop it there.

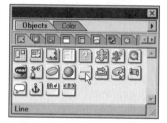

17.

Click below the line in the Layout Editor, and then drag an Image icon from the Objects palette into the Layout Editor.

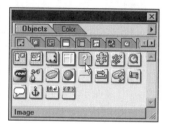

18.

Click to the right of the image icon in the Layout Editor, and then press Enter to move the text cursor down. Next, click on the Line icon in the Objects palette and drag a second line into the Layout Editor.

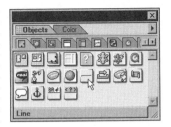

19.

Your page should now have a horizontal line, an empty image below it, and a second horizontal line below the image. The second horizontal line looks different from the first one because, being the last object added, it is currently selected.

20.

Click on the image icon in the Layout Editor. In the Image Inspector, enter a file name for the logo image. Alternatively, use the Point and Shoot button or the Browse button to select the image file.

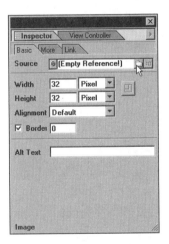

21.

While the image is still selected, click on the Center Alignment button in the toolbar.

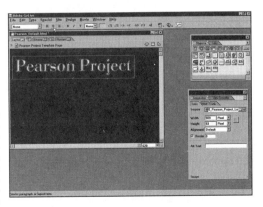

22.

The developing Web page should now look like this except, of course, that you are presumably using a different image for the company logo.

23.

Click below the second horizontal line, type "www.pearsonproject.com", and then highlight the text.

There is actually no such URL on the World Wide Web.

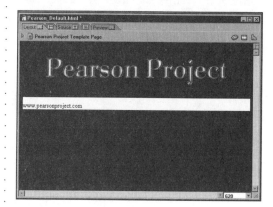

24.

We want this text to be larger than normal, so click on the Paragraph Format arrow in the toolbar and choose Header 3 from the drop-down list.

25.

To make it a different font face from the normal text, choose Type|Font|Arial from the menu.

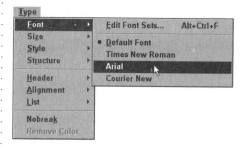

26.

Click on the Center Alignment button in the toolbar.

27.

In the Text Inspector, click on the New Link button.

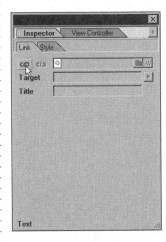

28.

Enter the URL you want to link to, or you can use the Point and Shoot button or the Browse button to select the file to link to.

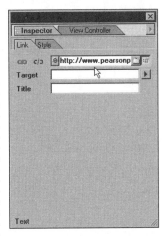

29.

In the Layout Editor, click to the right of the text and press Enter to drop down a line. Because the URL text is centered, the next line is also centered. To reset it to normal, click on the Left Alignment button in the toolbar.

30.

Click on the Line Break icon in the Objects palette. Drag it into the Layout Editor and drop it below the URL text. Press the Enter key to drop down a line.

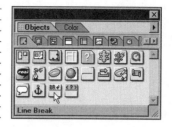

31.

Click on the Image icon in the Objects palette. Drag it into the Layout Editor and drop it below the Line Break. This will be a placeholder image only—each page in the site would show a different image in this spot.

32.

In the Image Inspector, click on the Alignment arrow and choose Abs Middle from the drop-down list. This will cause the center of any text that follows the image to align precisely with the center of the image.

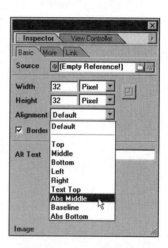

33.

Change the default border size from zero to 3.

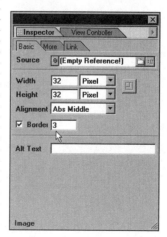

34.

In the Layout Editor, click to the right of the image. Type a space, and then type the words "Project Segment Image and description go here." Your page should now look like the figure on the right.

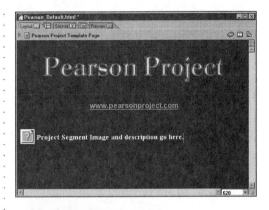

35.

Press Enter, and then click on the Line Break icon in the Objects palette. Drag it into the Layout Editor and drop it beneath the placeholder image.

36.

Click to the right of the Line Break, and then press Enter to drop down a line. To return the text size to normal for all subsequent text, click on the Paragraph Format arrow in the toolbar and choose None from the drop-down list.

37.

The template is now complete. Save the file, and then choose Edit|Preferences from the menu.

38.

Make sure that General is selected on the left side of the Preferences dialog box, and then click on the New Document checkbox so that it is selected.

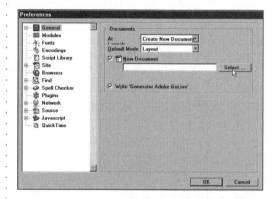

39.

Click on the Select button, navigate to the location where you have saved the template file, and then select it.

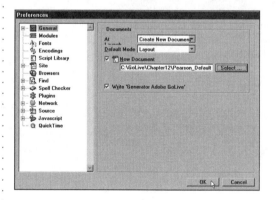

40.

Click on the OK button to complete the task. From now on, until you either deselect the New Document checkbox or select a different file for the default Web page, this file will be the one that will appear when you start GoLive or create a new page.

Project 2: Create a Navigation Bar Component

An HTML file that is intended to be embedded within another one is called a "component" in GoLive. In this project, you will create a navigation bar—a set of links to all the pages in a site—that can then be placed into every page to create a common method of moving about the site.

1.

Choose File|New Site|Blank from the menu.

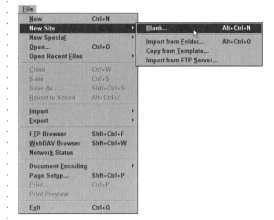

2.

Type "NavSite" over the default site name.

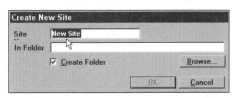

3.

Click on the Browse button and navigate to the folder you want to use to house the site.

If the folder doesn't exist, leave the Create Folder checkbox selected. Then you can just type the desired folder location into the In Folder text box.

4.

Click on the OK button.

5.

If the folder doesn't yet exist, you will be presented with a dialog box asking you to confirm that you want to create it. Click on the Yes button.

6.

The new site opens in GoLive. The Site Window shows the single Web page it contains by default—index.html.

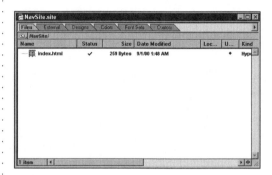

7.

Click on the Navigation View button in the toolbar.

8.

In Navigation View, click on the icon for index.html to select it.

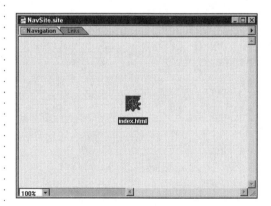

9.

Click on the New Child Page button in the toolbar.

It's the only New Page button that isn't grayed out at this point.

10.

The Navigation View now shows that index.html has a single child page, which is currently selected.

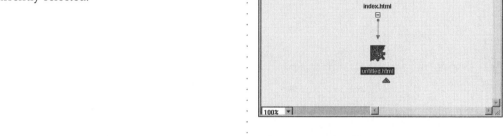

11.

In the File Inspector, highlight the default name "untitled.html" and replace it with "products.html".

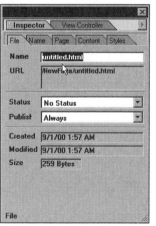

12.

Click on the New Next Page button in the toolbar.

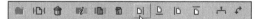

13.

Highlight the default Name and type "services.html" over it.

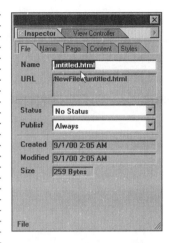

14.

The Navigation View now shows the three files, each appropriately named.

The yellow triangle beneath each of the new pages shows that they have no content yet.

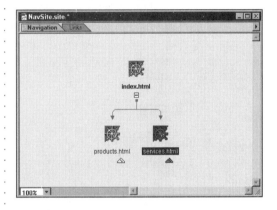

15.

Save the site, and then choose File|New from the menu to create a new Web page in the regular manner. This new page will not be added to the site in the same manner as the other two pages we just added, but will become a component instead.

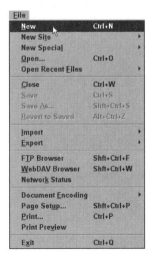

16.

Click on the Page icon on the upper left side of the Layout Editor.

17.

In the Page Inspector, highlight the title "Welcome to Adobe GoLive 5" and replace it by typing "Navigation Component" over it.

18.

Click on the HTML tab.

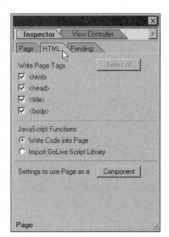

19.

Click on the Component button.

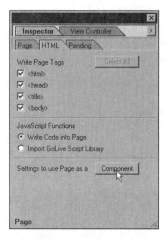

20.

Click on the Table icon in the Objects palette. Drag it into the Layout Editor and drop it there.

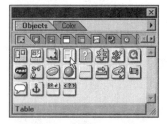

21.

Make sure the table is selected. In the Table Inspector, highlight the default value of 3 in the Rows text box and replace it by typing 1 over it.

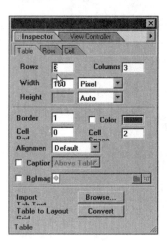

22.

Highlight the default value of zero in the Cell Pad text box and replace it by typing 4 over it. This keeps the text from coming right up against the sides of the cells, making it more easily readable.

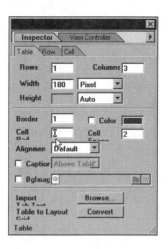

23.

Click within the first cell and type "Home", then hit Tab, and type "Products" in the second cell. Click Tab again and type "Services" in the third cell.

24.

Highlight the text in the first cell.

25.

In the Text Inspector, click on the New Link button.

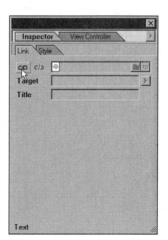

26.

Click on the Point and Shoot button and drag it into the Site Window. When the rubber band line touches index.html, release the mouse button to complete the link.

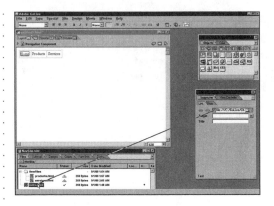

27.

Repeat Steps 24 through 26 for the second and third cells, linking them to products.html and services.html, respectively.

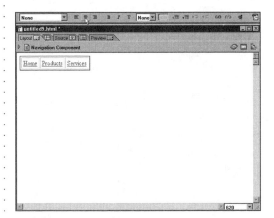

28.

Select the table and click on the Center Alignment button in the toolbar.

29.

Choose File|Save As from the menu.

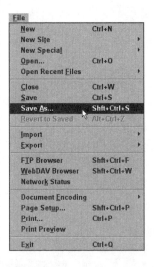

30.

Navigate to the site folder and give the file a name of "navigation_bar.html". DO NOT click on the Save button yet.

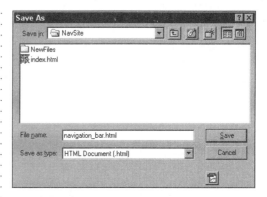

31.

Click on the pop-up menu button in the lower right corner of the dialog box.

It's on the top for Macs.

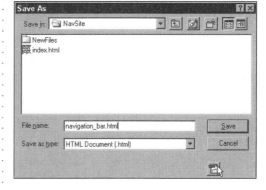

32.

Choose Components from the pop-up menu.

33.

The folder in the Save In box at the top of the dialog box automatically changes to Components, a special subfolder of the site. Click on the Save button to complete the process.

You can close navigation_bar.html now. It does not need to be opened in GoLive again unless you want to edit it.

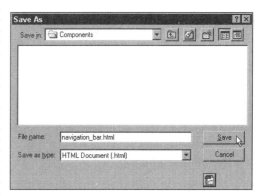

34.

When you want to add the new navigation bar component to any open page in this site, click on the Smart tab in the Objects palette.

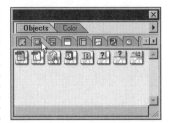

35.

Click on the Component icon, and then drag it into the Layout Editor and drop it there.

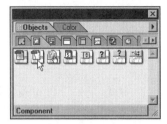

36.

In the Component Inspector, click on the Browse button.

37.

The Open dialog box will automatically go to the Components subfolder for this site. Double-click on the file name of the component you want to use, or you can click on it and then click on the Open button.

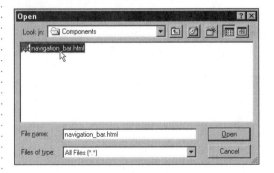

38.

The entire contents of the Web page you saved as a component will be inserted onto the new Web page.

| Home | Products | Services |

Project 3: Modify Source Code

Although GoLive is capable of handling most of the things you'll want to do with Web pages, it does have some limitations. You can do things in HTML that you can't do in GoLive. This short and simple project shows how to overcome some limitations in GoLive's handling of tables by manually changing the source code in the HTML Source Editor.

1.

Click on the Table icon in the Objects palette. Drag it into the Layout Editor and drop it there.

2.

The default table in GoLive is three rows of three cells each, and there is no native way to have more cells in one row than in another.

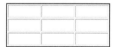

3.

Click on the Source tab to open the HTML Source Editor.

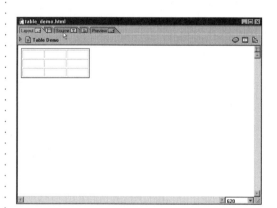

4.

Triple-click on one of the pairs of <td></td> tags to select the entire line.

```
<tr>
<td></td>
<td></td>
<td></td>
</tr>
```

5.

Choose Edit|Copy from the menu or use the key combination Ctrl+C (Command+C for Macs).

Edit	
Undo Marking	Ctrl+Z
Redo	Shft+Ctrl+Z
Cut	Ctrl+X
Copy	Ctrl+C
Paste	Ctrl+V
Delete	
Select All	Ctrl+A
Duplicate	Ctrl+D
Group	
Ungroup	
Find	Ctrl+F
Find Next	Ctrl+G
Find Selection	Ctrl+H
Replace	Ctrl+R
Replace & Find Next	Alt+Ctrl+R
Check Spelling...	Alt+Ctrl+U
Hide Invisible Items	Ctrl+I
Show Link Warnings	Shft+Ctrl+L
Web Settings...	Shft+Ctrl+Y
Adobe Online Settings...	
Keyboard Shortcuts...	Shft+Alt+Ctrl+K
Preferences...	Ctrl+Y

6.

Use your down-arrow key to drop down one line, and then choose Edit|Paste from the menu or use the key combination Ctrl+V (Command+V for Macs).

Edit	
Undo Copy	Ctrl+Z
Redo	Shft+Ctrl+Z
Cut	Ctrl+X
Copy	Ctrl+C
Paste	Ctrl+V
Delete	
Select All	Ctrl+A
Duplicate	Ctrl+D
Group	
Ungroup	
Find	Ctrl+F
Find Next	Ctrl+G
Find Selection	Ctrl+H
Replace	Ctrl+R
Replace & Find Next	Alt+Ctrl+R
Check Spelling...	Alt+Ctrl+U
Hide Invisible Items	Ctrl+I
Show Link Warnings	Shft+Ctrl+L
Web Settings...	Shft+Ctrl+Y
Adobe Online Settings...	
Keyboard Shortcuts...	Shft+Alt+Ctrl+K
Preferences...	Ctrl+Y

7.

The source code for the first table row now shows four cells.

```
<tr>
<td></td>
<td></td>
<td></td>
<td></td>
</tr>
```

8.

Click on the Layout tab and you will see that GoLive, which cannot display oddly sized table rows, now thinks that there are four cells in all the rows. The fourth cells in the second and third rows, however, are not really there, as you will see if you click on the Source tab and take a look at the source code.

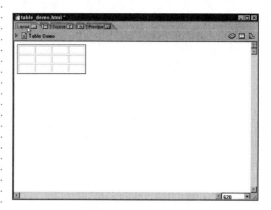

9.

Any time you use a program in a way it wasn't designed to be used, you must be careful of unforeseen problems. In this case, if you enter anything into the two "phantom" cells, GoLive will alter the source code and add them.

1A	2A	3A	4A
1B	2B	3B	4B
1C	2C	3C	4C

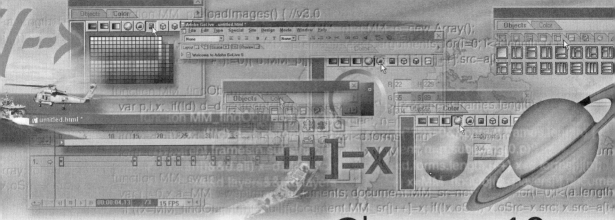

Chapter 13
Projects with Tables

Project 1: Make form fields line up
neatly by putting them in a table

Project 2: Create a title bar that
uses cell spanning

Getting the Most out of Tables

In Chapter 8, you learned how to create tables in GoLive.

In this chapter, you'll apply that knowledge to some common real-world situations.

Project 1: Tidy Form Fields

Forms are an important part of many Web pages, but they're also a bit on the sloppy side—unless you give them a little help. In this project, you'll set up a typical form that has labels, set up form controls, and then use a table to align the elements neatly.

1.

Click on the Forms tab in the Objects palette.

2.

Place your text cursor where you want the form to appear, and then double-click on the Form icon (or drag the Form icon onto the Web page).

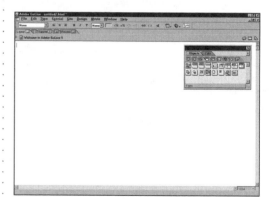

3.

Click on the Basic tab of the Objects palette, and then drag the Table icon into the form.

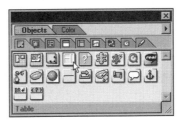

4.

If the Table Inspector isn't showing, choose Window|Inspector from the menu.

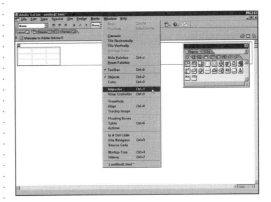

5.

In the Table Inspector, change the table settings to accommodate your form. Typically, this means two columns and enough rows to hold all the form controls. (We'll be using three rows in this project.) Make sure the table is wide enough, also.

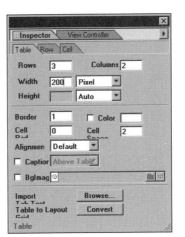

6.

Set the border size to 0 (zero) so that the table won't show. Set cell padding and/or cell spacing to provide the desired distance between the form controls.

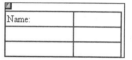

7.

Click within the first table cell and type "Name" to describe the first control.

8.

Click on the Forms tab in the Objects palette and drag a text box into the second table cell.

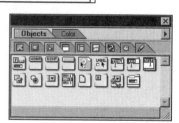

9.

In the second row, type "Password" in the first cell and drag a Password icon from the Forms tab into the second cell. Drag a Submit button into the second cell of the third row.

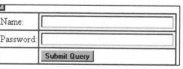

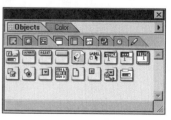

10.

Shift+click on the top of the first column to select it.

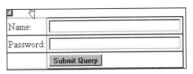

11.

In the Cell Inspector, set the horizontal alignment to Right.

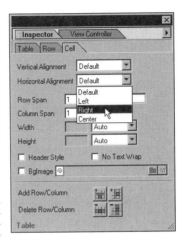

12.

Shift+click on the top of the second column to select it.

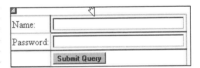

13.

In the Cell Inspector, set the horizontal alignment to Left. Save the Web page.

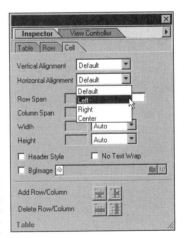

14.

Preview your form in all target Web browsers and make any necessary adjustments to the table settings to achieve the exact appearance you desire.

Project 2: Titles That Use Cell Spanning

Cell spanning—the ability of a single cell to stretch across more than one column or row— is most useful for setting descriptive titles.

1.

Click on the Basic tab of the Objects palette, and then drag the Table icon into the Layout Editor.

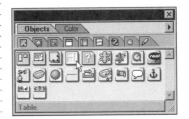

2.

If the Table Inspector isn't showing, choose Window|Inspector from the menu.

3.

Set the table to be 4 columns wide by 4 rows high.

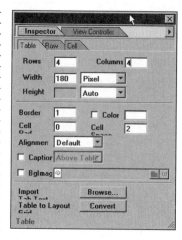

4.

Select the third cell in the first row.

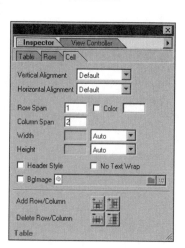

5.

Click on the Cell tab in the Table Inspector and set that cell to have a column span of 2.

6.

Set the cell to have a horizontal alignment of Center.

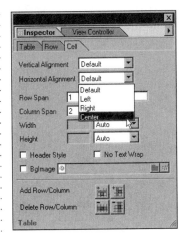

7.

Click within the expanded cell and type "Competition".

8.

Click within the third cell in the second row and type "A Team".

9.

Select that cell and set it to a horizontal alignment of Center.

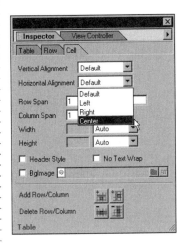

10.

Click within the fourth cell in the second row and type "B Team".

11.

Select that cell and set it to a horizontal alignment of Center.

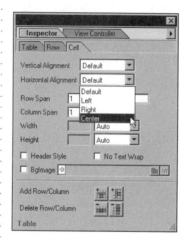

12.

Select the first cell in the third row.

13.

Set that cell to have a row span of 2.

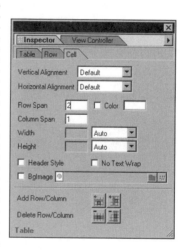

14.

Click within the expanded cell and type "Rounds".

15.

Click within the second cell in the third row and type "1".

	Competition	
	A Team	B Team
Rounds	1	

16.

Select that cell and set it to a horizontal alignment of Right.

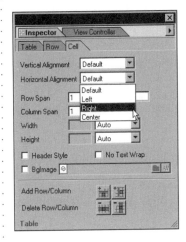

17.

Click within the second cell in the fourth row and type "2".

	Competition	
	A Team	B Team
Rounds	1	
	2	

18.

Select that cell and set it to a horizontal alignment of Right.

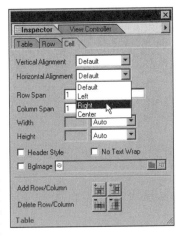

19.

Click within the third cell in the third row and type "27".

	Competition	
	A Team	B Team
Rounds	1	27<
	2	

20.

Select that cell and set it to a horizontal alignment of Right.

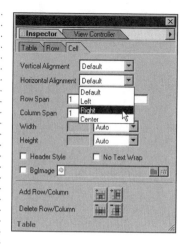

21.

Click within the fourth cell in the third row and type "38".

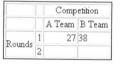

22.

Select that cell and set it to a horizontal alignment of Right.

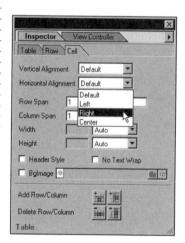

23.

Click within the third cell in the final row and type "42".

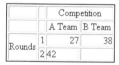

24.

Select that cell and set it to a horizontal alignment of Right.

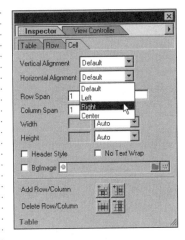

25.

Click within the fourth cell in the final row and type "73".

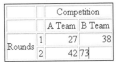

26.

Select that cell and set it to a horizontal alignment of Right.

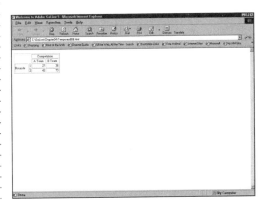

27.

Preview your form in all target Web browsers and make any necessary adjustments to the table settings to achieve the exact appearance you desire.

Although the empty cells will not show cell borders, the table border still outlines where they are; there is no way to get rid of this undesired effect.

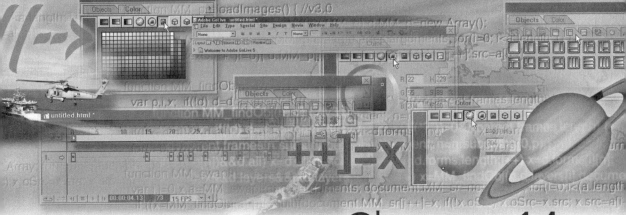

Chapter 14
Projects with Frames

 Project 1: Create a Navigation Frame

 Project 2: Work with targets

 Project 3: Add NOFRAMES content

Getting the Most out of Frames

Frames are among the most versatile and useful tools at your disposal. In this chapter, we'll take a look at how to put them to some practical uses—and how to cope with a few flukes in GoLive's handling of frames, too.

Project 1: Create a Navigation Frame

Frames are a very popular method for providing easy site navigation to visitors. Because a navigation bar or set of links in a side, top, or bottom frame will stay put no matter what happens in other frames, this is a common way to present navigation information.

1.

Click on the Frame Editor tab in the Document Window.

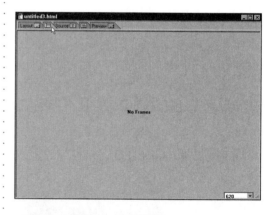

2.

Click on the Frames tab of the Objects palette.

3.

Click on the frame set design that most closely approximates the one you want to create. In this example, we're using a left-side navigation frame.

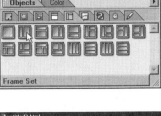

4.

Drag the icon into the Frame Editor and drop it there.

5.

Click within the left-hand frame. This is the frame that will end up holding the navigation page.

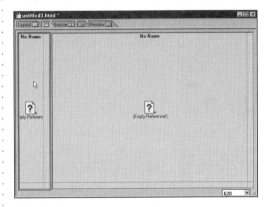

6.

In the Frame Inspector, highlight the default name and type "Navigation" over it.

7.

Click within the right-hand frame. This is the frame that will be used to display the files that are selected in the Navigation frame.

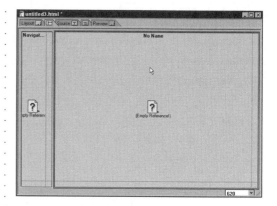

8.

In the Frame Inspector, highlight the default name and type "Display" over it.

9.

The Frame Editor has no provision for setting page properties, so you need to click on the Layout tab.

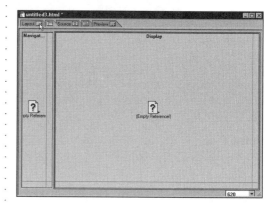

10.

In Layout view, click on the Page icon to open the Page Inspector.

11.

In the Page Inspector, highlight the default title and type your own title for the frame set over it.

Remember, the title has nothing to do with the frame names. This is the overall page name that will be shown at the top of a Web browser when people visit the framed pages.

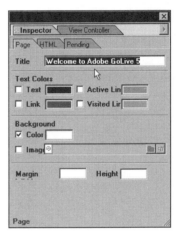

12.

Select File|Save As from the menu and save the frame set as index.html.

A frame set, like any other HTML file, can have any name at all. The frame set in this project, however, serves as the main page of a Web site.

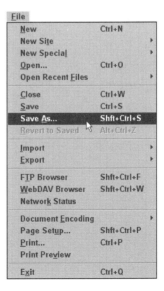

13.

Open a new file and type in the text for the links you want to have in your navigation frame. Save the file as Nav_Links.html.

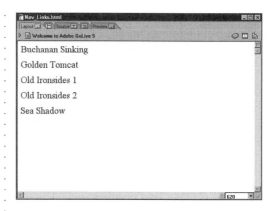

14.

Highlight the first line of text and click on the Create New Link button in the Text Inspector (or the same button on the toolbar).

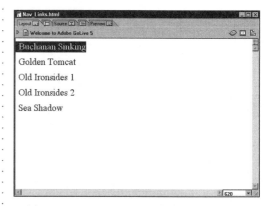

15.

In the Text Inspector, use the Point and Shoot button or the Browse button to designate which file to link to, or you can highlight the words [Empty Reference!] and type the file name over them.

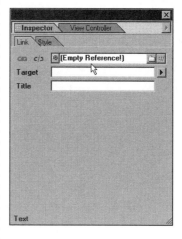

16.

Click on the arrow to the right of the Target text box and select Display from the drop-down list of available targets.

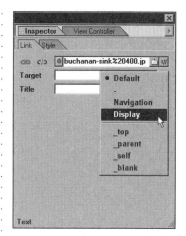

You could also just type "Display" into the Target text box. Using the drop-down list, however, helps avoid any typographical errors.

Repeat Steps 14 through 16 for each link until all are completed. Save the file again to preserve your changes.

17.

Bring up the frame set (index.html) and click within the Navigation frame.

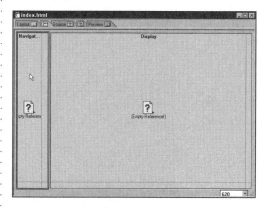

18.

In the Frame Inspector, use the Point and Shoot button or the Browse button to link to Nav_Links.html, or you can highlight the words [Empty Reference!] and type "Nav_Links.html" over them.

19.

Because framed pages do not show in the Frame Editor, you need to click on the Preview tab to see the results of your actions.

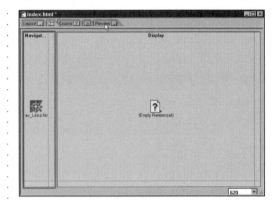

20.

The Display frame shows an error message simply because no file has been linked to it yet. The links in the Navigation frame do not fit, so that frame will need to be resized.

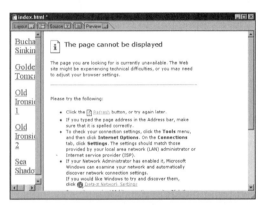

21.

Unfortunately, you cannot resize the frame while you view its content, so you have to click on the Frame Editor tab again. Back in the Frame Editor, click on the border between the two frames and drag it to the right.

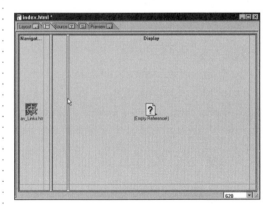

22.

Click on the Preview tab to see the results of the frame resizing. Repeat Steps 19 through 21 as many times as necessary to get the layout you want.

You can also adjust the font size in the Nav_Links.html file to help fit the links into the available space.

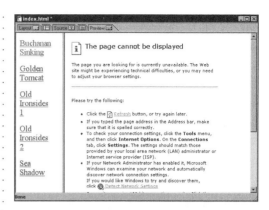

23.

In the Frame Editor, click within the Display frame.

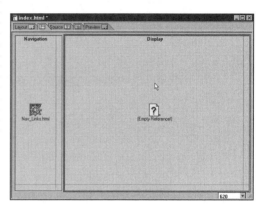

24.

In the Frames Inspector, select a file for the Display frame by using the Point and Shoot button, typing a reference, or using the Browse button. This will be the default file that shows when the frame is first loaded.

25.

Click on the Preview tab to view the results. In this case, we've chosen to use the image file from the first link in Nav_Links.html instead of using an HTML file.

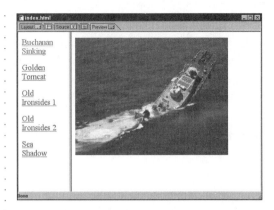

26.

Clicking on the links in Preview mode does nothing when you're using frames in GoLive. The same frame set viewed in a Web browser, however, works fine.

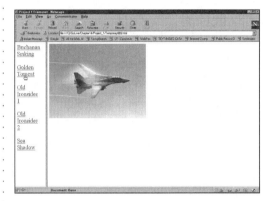

Project 2: Work with Targets

The preceding project used a simple target—a named frame—but this is just scratching the surface. There are several built-in targets that you can use to advantage, including one that opens a second instance of a visitor's Web browser. In this project, we'll start with the same type of layout as before and progress to using a nested frame set to explore all the variations.

1.

Open the frame set created in Project 1, and then choose File|Save As from the menu and save it as "Top_Frameset.html".

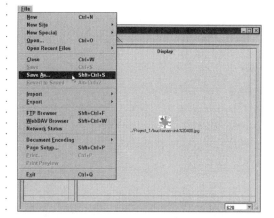

2.

Click within the left-hand frame. In the Frame Inspector, highlight the name and type "Left" over it.

3.

Click within the right-hand frame. In the Frame Inspector, highlight the name and type "Right" over it. Change the page title if desired (see Steps 9 through 12 in Project 1). Save the file to preserve the changes.

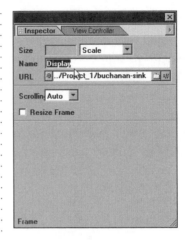

4.

Open a new file and type in the following text, each on a separate line: "Default", "Dash", "Top", "Parent", "Self", and "Blank". Save the file as "Target_Test.html".

5.

Highlight the first line of text and click on the Create New Link button in the Text Inspector (or the same button on the toolbar).

6.

In the Text Inspector, use the Point and Shoot button or the Browse button to designate which file to link to, or you can highlight the words [Empty Reference!] and type the file name over them.

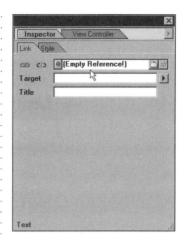

You might find it simpler to use the same file to link to from all the links. You may also wish to resize the frames, depending upon what you link to.

7.

Click on the arrow to the right of the Target text box and select Default from the drop-down list of available targets.

Repeat Steps 5 through 7 for each link until all are completed, selecting "-" for the target for Dash, "_top" for the target for Top, and so forth, matching each target to the appropriate text. Save the file again to preserve your changes.

8.

Bring up the frame set (Top_Frameset.html) and click within the Left frame. In the Frame Inspector, use the Point and Shoot button or the Browse button to link to Target_Test.html, or you can highlight the words [Empty Reference!] and type "Target_Test.html" over them. Repeat for the Right frame with the same file. Save the frame set to preserve the changes.

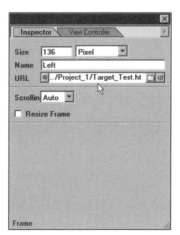

9.

Open Top_Frameset.html in a Web browser and click on the first link (Default) in the Left frame. Use the Back button in your browser and then click on the same link in the Right frame. Repeat for all links to get a feel for the function of each target.

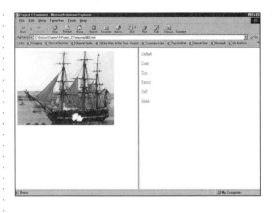

The "-" target is a GoLive oddity. It's not a legal target name (only names that begin with alphanumeric characters and the four special targets that begin with "_" are allowed). Netscape treats it as a _self link; Internet Explorer properly treats it as a bogus name and opens the link in a separate window.

10.

Back in GoLive, click on Top_Frameset.html, and then choose File|Save As from the menu and save it under the new name of "Nesting_Frameset.html".

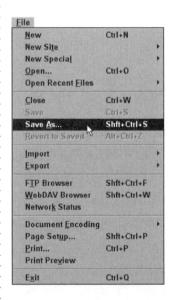

11.

Click on the border between the two frames to select the frame set.

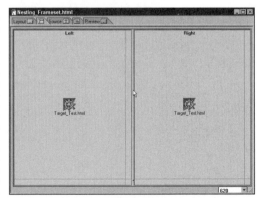

12.

In the Frame Set Inspector, click on the Vertical radio button to change the orientation of the frames.

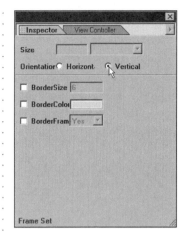

13.

Click in the top frame. In the Frame Inspector, highlight the name and type "NestedTop" over it. Do the same with the bottom frame, typing the new name "NestedBottom". Save the file to preserve the changes.

14.

Choose File|Open Recent Files from the menu and reopen Top_Frameset.html.

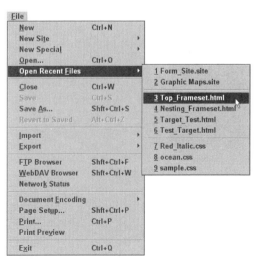

15.

Click within the Right frame. In the Frame Inspector, use the Point and Shoot button or the Browse button to link to Nesting_Frameset.html, or you can highlight the words [Empty Reference!] and type "Nesting_Frameset.html" over them. Save the file to preserve the changes.

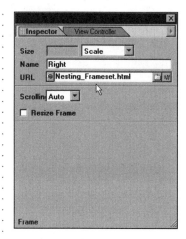

16.

Open Top_Frameset.html in a Web browser. The Right frame is filled with the file Nesting_Frameset.html.

17.

All links work as before, except the one that has the _parent target; the reason is that the parent of the two frames in the Right frame is the Right frame, not Top_Frameset.html. Clicking on the Parent link in either of the nested frames opens a file in the Right frame only.

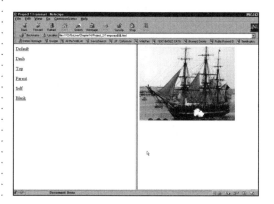

Project 3: Add NOFRAMES Content

The overwhelming majority of Web surfers (those who use recent versions of Netscape Navigator or Internet Explorer) can see frames. However, plenty of people use old versions of the major browsers or use other methods of surfing the Web. The NOFRAMES element is HTML's solution to this problem. Unfortunately, GoLive doesn't offer any NOFRAMES options in the Frames Inspector.

1.

Open a frame set, and then click on the Source tab to access the HTML Source Code Editor.

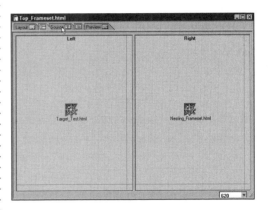

2.

GoLive provides a NOFRAMES element, but it's not in the right place. To conform to proper HTML, highlight it and drag it into the FRAMESET element.

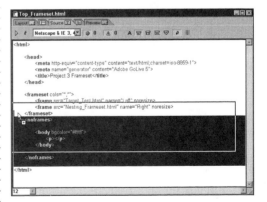

3.

Drop the NOFRAMES element within the FRAMESET element.

A NOFRAMES element can exist only within a frame set. Putting it anywhere else will cause your page to fail any HTML validation test.

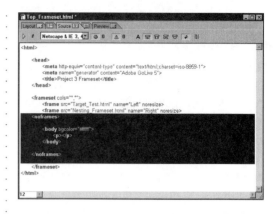

4.

Between the <BODY> and </BODY> tags, enter the HTML content that you want users who don't have frames-capable browsers to see.

```
<noframes>
<body bgcolor=□#ffffff□>
<p></p>
</body>
</noframes>
```

5.

Many Webmasters simply add a comment to the effect that anyone reading this message is using a defective Web browser and should download the Webmaster's favorite one instead. This approach is unlikely to win friends for you.

To provide a better solution, copy the source code from your navigation frame and paste it here.

```
<noframes>
<body bgcolor=□#ffffff□>
<p><a href=□iron2000_400.jpg□>Default</a></p>
<p><a href=□sail_100.jpg□ target=□-□>Dash</a>
</p>
<p><a href=□goldtom_400.jpg□ target=□_top□>
Top</a></p>
<p><a href=□seashadow_400.jpg□
 target=□_parent□>Parent</a></p>
</body>
</noframes>
```

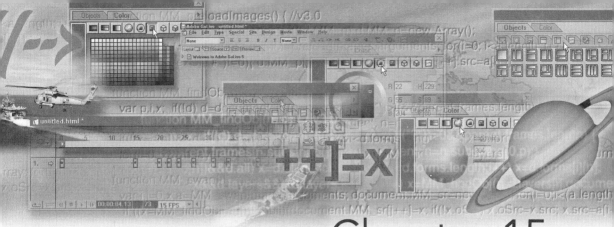

Chapter 15
Projects with
JavaScript Actions

  Project 1: Open alert windows

  Project 2: Initialize and set variables

  Project 3: Change background color

Taking Action with Scripts

The projects in this chapter explore several different aspects of using GoLive's JavaScript actions. Each one combines two or more important techniques that you can use to improve your Web pages' usage of actions.

Project 1: Open Alert Windows

JavaScript alert windows are a commonly used method of presenting information to your site's visitors. This project uses normal text to supply the messages in the alert windows. It also uses the OnLoad and OnUnload triggers to show how actions can be made to take place as different events occur.

1.

Create two blank Web pages. Give one a file name of "project1a.html" and the other one a file name of "project1b.html." Close project1b.html—its only purpose is to provide a destination for a link.

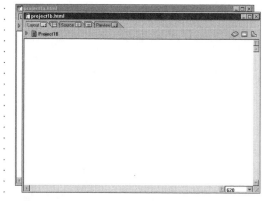

2.

Click on the Toggle Head Section button to open the Head section of project1a.html.

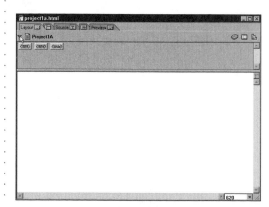

3.

Click on the Smart tab in the Objects palette.

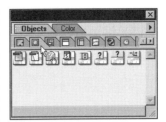

4.

Click on the Head Action icon and drag it into the Head section of project1a.html.

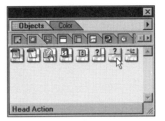

5.

Drag a second Head Action item into the Head section.

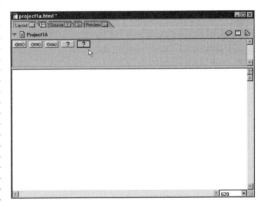

6.

Select the first Head Action item. In the Action Inspector, click on the Action button.

We want this particular action to trigger immediately upon the opening of the Web page, so we leave the Exec. setting at OnLoad.

In the Actions menu, choose Message|Open Alert Window.

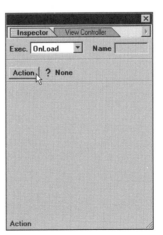

7.

Back in the Action Inspector, highlight the default Message text and type the phrase "Welcome to my site!" over it.

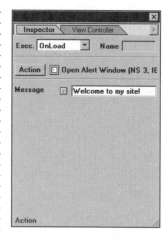

8.

Select the second Head Action item. In the Action Inspector, click on the Exec. drop-down list and choose OnUnload.

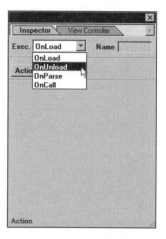

This option means that the action will not take place until the visitor is leaving the page to go elsewhere.

9.

Click on the Action button to bring up the menu.

Choose Message|Open Alert Window from the menu.

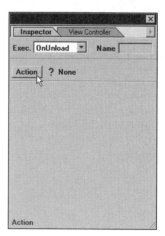

10.

Highlight the default Message text and type "Goodbye!" over it.

11.

Type the words "LEAVE THE PAGE" in the Body section. Select the phrase so that it is highlighted.

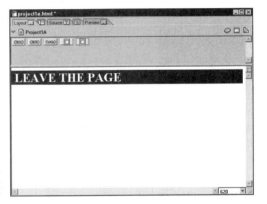

12.

In the Text Inspector, click on the New Link button.

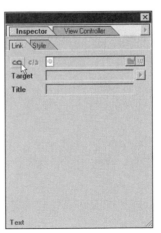

13.

Click on the Browse button and select the file project1b.html as the link.

You can, of course, link to anything you want to. We use a blank local page for simplicity.

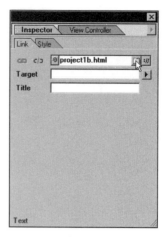

14.

Save project1a.html, and then click on the Show In Browser button and select a test browser.

It's a good idea to test any JavaScript action in at least both major Web browsers.

15.

When the page loads, the first alert window will be displayed. Click on OK to proceed.

16.

Click on the link to exit the page.

17.

The second alert window pops up. Click on OK to complete exiting the page.

Project 2: Initialize and Set Variables

This project uses alert windows to show the current state of a variable. It also shows how multiple actions can be assigned to a single trigger. In this case, three different actions will be caused by one mouse click.

1.

Create a Web page named "Project2.html".

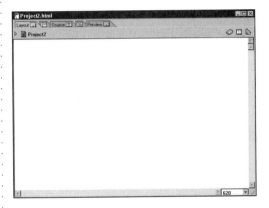

2.

Click on the Toggle Head Section button to open the Head.

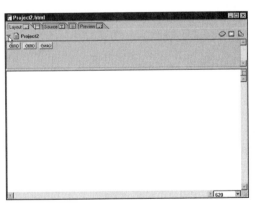

3.

Click on the Smart tab in the Objects palette.

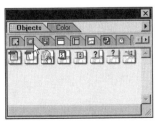

4.

Click on the Head Action icon and drag it into the Head section.

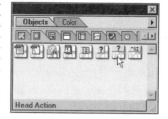

5.

Drag a second Head Action item into the Head section.

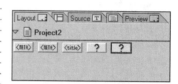

6.

Select the first Head Action item. In the Action Inspector, click on the Action button.

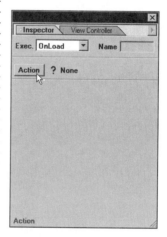

7.

Choose Variables|Declare Variable from the Action menu. Declaring a variable creates it.

It is critical for the Head Action item that has the declaration to come first. If the variable has not been created, its value cannot exist either.

8.

Enter "Var01" in the Name text box. Click on the Type arrow and select String from the drop-down list, because this will be a textual variable.

Normally, a variable name should be descriptive of the function it performs to clearly distinguish it from other variables. Because we are dealing with only one variable here, we have used a generic name instead.

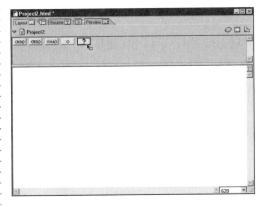

9.

Click on the second Head Action item. This is the one that will be used to set the initial value of the variable that was created in the first Head Action item.

10.

In the Action Inspector, click on the Action button to bring up the menu.

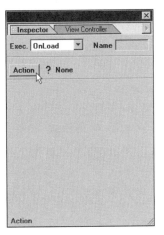

11.

Choose Variables|Init Variable from the menu.

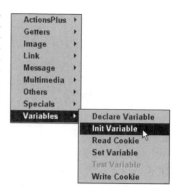

12.

Click on the Variable arrow and select the variable from the drop-down list.

If you have created many variables, they will all be listed here, of course.

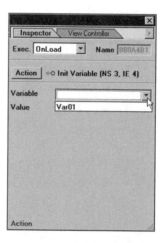

13.

Type the word "INITIALIZED" into the Value text box.

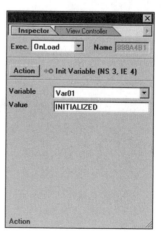

14.

Type the words "READ AND SET VALUE" in the Body section. Select the phrase so that it is highlighted.

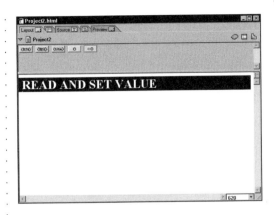

15.

In the Text Inspector, click on the New Link button.

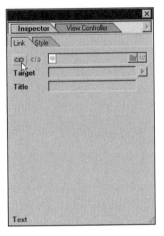

16.

Because this link is only being created so that an action can be keyed to it, enter a hash mark (#) as the URL.

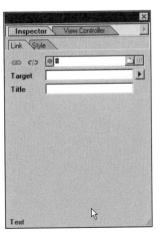

17.

In the Actions palette, Mouse Click is the default event. Leave that as is and click on the New Action button three times.

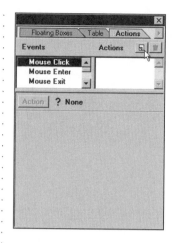

18.

Select the first unspecified action, and then click on the Action button to bring up the menu.

19.

Choose Message|Open Alert Window from the menu.

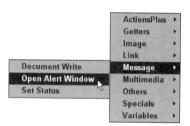

20.

Instead of typing in a message, click on the red C.

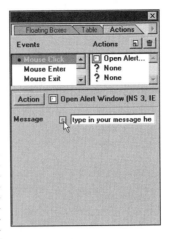

21.

A blue ball will replace the red C. Click on the Message arrow and select the variable from the drop-down list. This alert window will show the value of the variable when the page is first loaded.

This option, of course, is not available unless at least one variable has been declared.

22.

Select the next unspecified action, and then click on the Action button to bring up the menu.

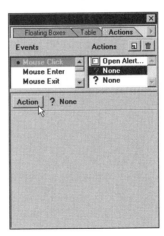

23.

Choose Variables|Set Variable from the menu.

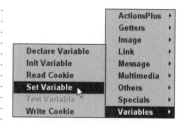

24.

Click on the Variable arrow and choose the variable from the drop-down list.

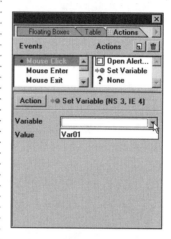

25.

Type the word "CHANGED" into the Value text box. This will be the new value after the mouse-click trigger takes place.

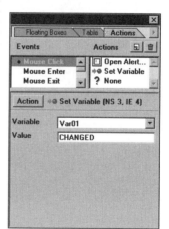

26.

Select the remaining unspecified action, and then click on the Action button to bring up the menu.

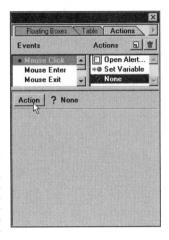

27.

Choose Message|Open Alert Window from the menu.

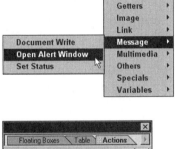

28.

Click on the red C next to the Message box.

29.

Click on the Message arrow and choose the variable from the drop-down list. This alert window will show the value of the variable after the Set Variable action takes place.

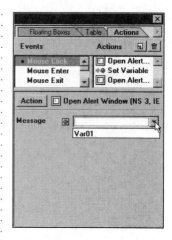

30.

Save project2.html, and then click on the Show In Browser button and select a test browser.

It's a good idea to test any JavaScript action in at least both major Web browsers.

31.

Click on the text.

READ AND SET VALUE

32.

The first alert window pops up, displaying the value of the variable at the time of page loading—its initial value. Click on OK.

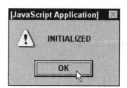

33.

The second and third actions take place, setting a new value for the variable and displaying that value in a new alert window.

If you click on the text again at this point, both alert windows will display "CHANGED." The value "INITIALIZED" is only created when the page is loaded.

Project 3: Change Background Color

This project uses a simple action to show how to use multiple triggers with a single object and how to toggle a result back and forth. It also uses a text link embedded in a button to launch the actions.

1.

Create a new Web page and name it "Project3.html".

2.

Click on the Forms tab of the Objects palette.

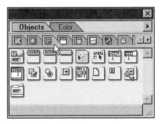

3.

Double-click on the Form icon to place a form on the Web page.

4.

Drag the Button icon into the form on the Web page.

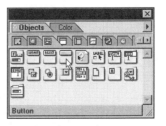

5.

Highlight the word "Button" in the middle of the form button.

It isn't always easy to do this with the mouse. You might want to try clicking on the text, and then using your Shift key and arrow keys to highlight it.

6.

Type the words "CHANGE COLOR" over the default text.

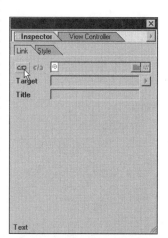

Even though it's in a button, this text can be styled like any other text on a Web page. Here, we have made it Arial, size 7, and bold.

7.

Click on the New Link button in the Text Inspector.

8.

Because we don't need this to actually link to anything, type a hash mark (#) as the URL.

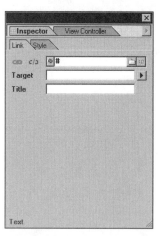

9.

Every mouse click consists of two events—a Mouse Down and a Mouse Up. We're going to use both of them individually. Scroll down in the Events listing and select Mouse Down. Click on the New Action button.

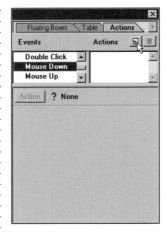

10.

Click on the Action button to open the menu.

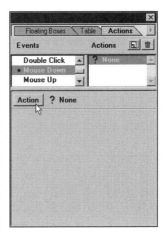

11.

Choose Others|Set BackColor from the menu. This action is used to change the background color of the Web page.

12.

Click on the color box.

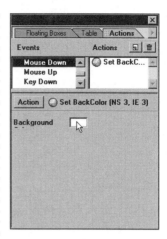

13.

Use the Color palette to choose the new background color.

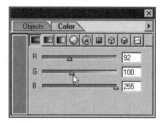

We're using the slider bars here, but any of the Color palette's methods will do. Use whichever one you're most comfortable with.

14.

To set up the next trigger, select Mouse Up in the Events listing. Click on the New Action button.

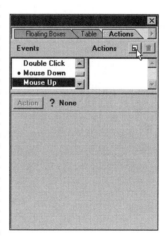

Notice that Mouse Down has a bullet next to it. You can quickly check which events are active by scrolling down the Events listing and looking for bullets.

15.

Click on the Action button to bring up the menu.

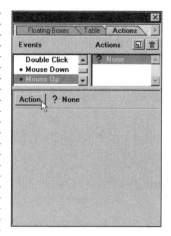

16.

Choose Others|Set BackColor from the menu. This time, however, do not set any background color. Just leave it at the default white.

17.

Save project3.html, and then click on the Show In Browser button and select a test browser.

It's a good idea to test any JavaScript action in at least both major Web browsers.

18.

The Web page loads with its default white background color.

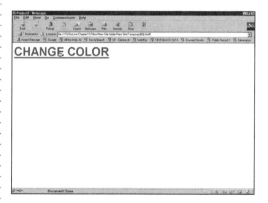

19.

Click on the text and keep holding the mouse button down. The Mouse Down action takes place, changing the white background color to the new color.

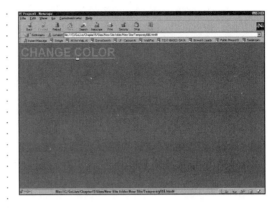

20.

Release the mouse button and the Mouse Up action takes place, changing the background color back to the default white.

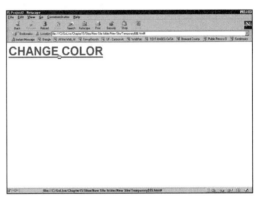

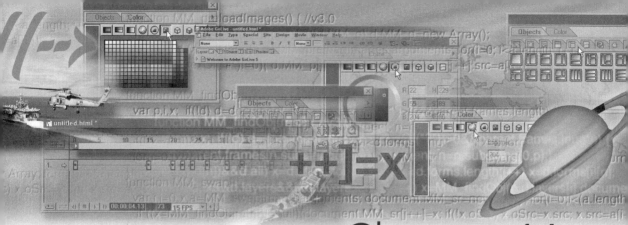

Chapter 16
Projects with Animation

Project 1: Move a floating box

Project 2: Use visibility and depth

Project 3: Add actions to a timeline

Exploring Timelines

The Timeline Editor is the key to using GoLive to create dynamic Web pages. It gives you the ability to control not only the position of floating boxes, but their attributes as well. These can be set at the starting, transitional, and ending points of any timeline.

Project 1: Move a Floating Box

This project explores the four different animation methods used to move floating boxes around a Web browser's screen.

1.

Create a Web page named "animation01.html".

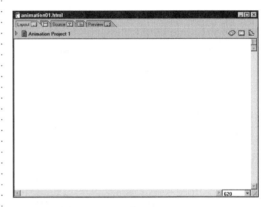

2.

In the Basic tab of the Objects palette, click on the Floating Box icon.

3.

Drag the icon into the Layout Editor and drop it there. Click on one of its edges to select it.

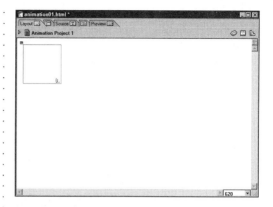

4.

In the Floating Box Inspector, click on the Animation arrow and choose None from the drop-down list. Make a note of the original Left and Top positions of the floating box—in the final step of this project, you will enter those figures to return the floating box to its starting point.

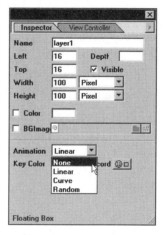

5.

In the Basic tab of the Objects palette, click on the Image icon.

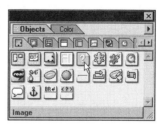

6.

Drag the icon into the floating box within the Layout Editor and drop it there.

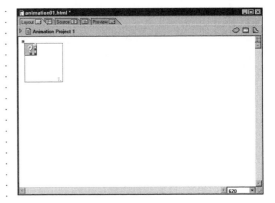

7.

In the Image Inspector, enter the file name, or you can use the Point and Shoot button or the Browse button to select the image file to be contained within the floating box.

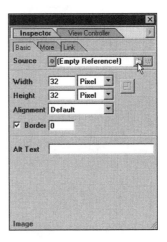

8.

Click on the Open DHTML Timeline Editor button at the top right of the Layout Editor (the one in the center that looks like a filmstrip).

When the Timeline Editor comes up, it may be covered by other palettes. If so, you'll need to move them.

9.

In the Timeline Editor, Ctrl+click at the point where you want the next stage of the animation to take place. Mac users Command+click instead.

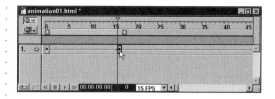

You don't have to be precise in your initial placement. If the marker is not where you want it, you can simply click on it and drag it to a new location.

10.

The default timing of animations in GoLive is 15 frames per second, so if you want the next stage of the animation to take place one second after the page opens, place the marker at 15 on the upper scale. If you want to change the default value for the number of frames per second, click on the arrow next to "15 FPS" and select the desired value from the drop-down list.

11.

Place the mouse pointer on any side of the floating box. When you get a hand shape, hold down the mouse button and drag the floating box into a new position.

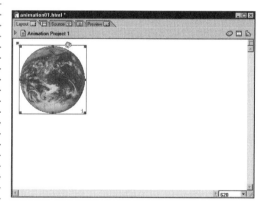

12.

Because "None" is the chosen method of animation, no connection is shown between the original position and the second position. When the animation executes, the floating box will move between the first and second positions without any transitional stages—in other words, it will simply jump from Point A to Point B at the specified time.

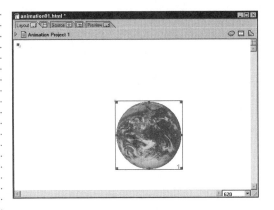

13.

In the Floating Box Inspector, select Linear from the Animation drop-down list.

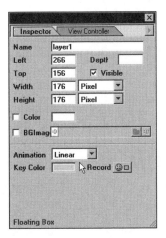

14.

Ctrl+click at the third animation point. Mac users use Command+click.

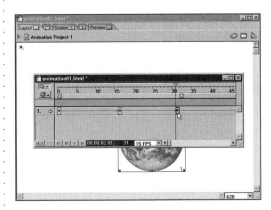

15.

Place the mouse pointer on any side of the floating box. When you get a hand shape, hold down the mouse button and drag the floating box into a new position.

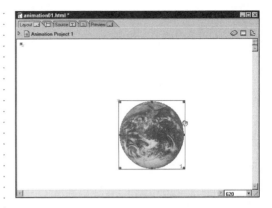

16.

Because Linear is the chosen method of animation, a line is shown between the second position and the third position. When the animation executes, the floating box will move between the second and third positions in a direct line.

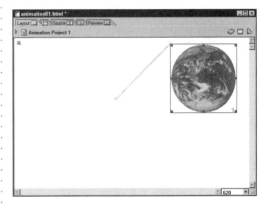

17.

In the Floating Box Inspector, click on the Animation arrow and choose Curve from the drop-down list.

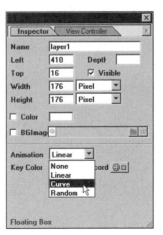

18.

Ctrl+click at the fourth animation point. Mac users use Command+click.

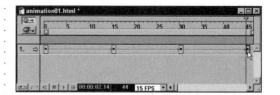

19.

Once again, place the mouse pointer on any side of the floating box. When you get a hand shape, hold down the mouse button and drag the floating box into a new position.

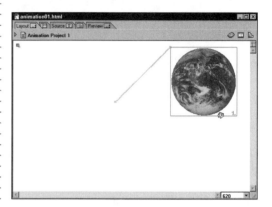

20.

Because Curve is the chosen method of animation, an arc is shown between the second position and the third position. When the animation executes, the floating box will move between the third and fourth positions in a curving motion.

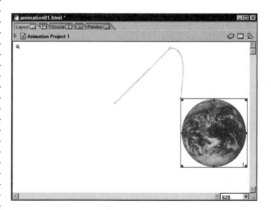

21.

In the Floating Box Inspector, click on the Animation arrow and choose Random from the drop-down list.

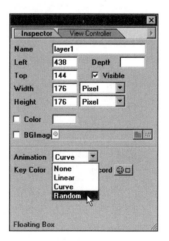

22.

Ctrl+click at the fifth animation point. Mac users use Command+click.

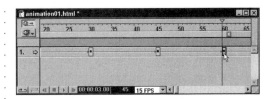

Use the scrollbar at the bottom right of the Timeline Editor to get to more of the timeline. Alternatively, resize or maximize the Timeline Editor.

23.

Back in Step 4, you wrote down the coordinates that the floating box originated from. Enter them now in the Left and Top text boxes in the Floating Box Inspector.

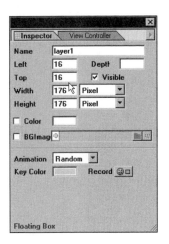

24.

Because Random is the chosen method of animation, a line that dissolves into a crazy scribble (behind the image) is shown. When the animation executes, the floating box will jump all over the screen as it moves between the fourth and fifth positions, returning to its origin point.

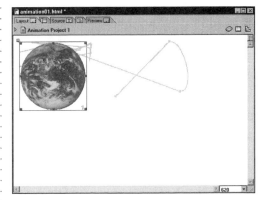

25.

Save the file, and then click on the Preview tab to view the animation in action.

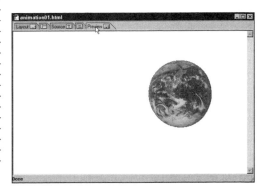

Project 2: Use Visibility and Depth

This project uses two different floating boxes that are the same size and in the same position. The depth setting determines which one is on top of the other; visibility is used to turn the top one on and off, alternately revealing and concealing the bottom one.

1.

Create a Web page named "animation02.html".

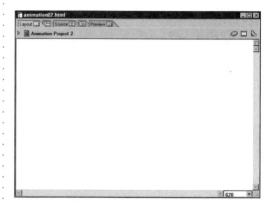

2.

In the Basic tab of the Objects palette, click on the Floating Box icon.

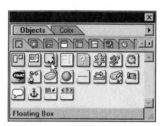

3.

Drag the icon into the Layout Editor and drop it there.

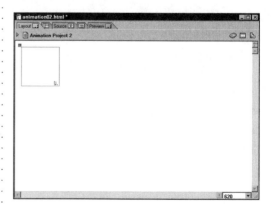

You can also double-click on the icon instead of dragging and dropping it.

4.

Add a second floating box. The two boxes overlap. To make the work easier, drag the second floating box to the side so that they do not overlap.

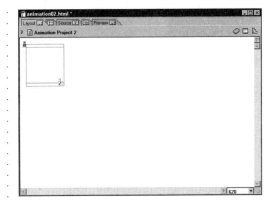

5.

Type the word "SALE" into the first floating box and the words "TODAY ONLY" into the second one.

6.

Click within the text and then select Header 1 from the Paragraph Format drop-down menu in the toolbar.

7.

The second floating box expands to accommodate the size of its contents.

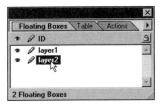

You may want to center the text as we have done here, but it is not necessary.

8.

It's a bit tricky to select a floating box by clicking on the tiny anchor associated with it on the left side of the Web page. A far easier approach is to click on the name of the floating box in the Floating Boxes palette.

If the Floating Boxes palette isn't open, choose Window|Floating Boxes from the menu.

9.

Note the width of the larger floating box in the Floating Box palette.

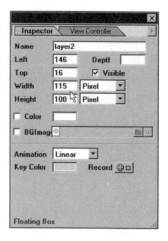

10.

Select the smaller floating box by clicking on its name in the Floating Boxes palette.

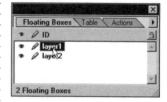

11.

Highlight the Width setting in the Floating Box Inspector and type the value from the larger box over it. In this case, you would change the 100 to 115. Also, write down the Top and Left settings for the first box; you'll need them later.

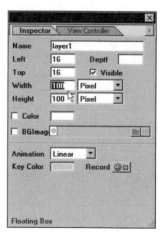

12.

Both floating boxes are now the same size, so that when one is placed on top of the other, it will completely cover it.

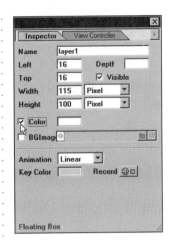

13.

In the Floating Box Inspector, click on the Color checkbox. This adds a white background color to the floating box; otherwise, it will be transparent and will show the contents of the Web page that lies underneath it. Do the same for the other floating box as well.

You can, of course, click on the Color box to the right and select a color other than white.

14.

Select the second floating box and, in the Floating Box Inspector, change its Left setting (and Top setting, if necessary) so that it perfectly overlaps the first one.

15.

The second floating box completely obscures the first one. The most recently added floating box will always lie on top of any earlier ones unless you specify a different stacking order.

16.

To change the stacking order, enter a value of 1 in the Depth text box in the Floating Box Inspector for the second floating box. Select the first floating box and enter a value of 2 in its Depth text box.

17.

The first floating box is now on top of the second one. The one that has the higher depth setting will always be on top of ones that have lower depth values.

18.

Click on the Open DHTML Timeline Editor button at the top right of the Layout Editor (the one in the center that looks like a filmstrip).

19.

The Timeline Editor shows two different tracks—one for each floating box. The arrow on the first track shows that it is the currently active one.

20.

Ctrl+click at the 5-frame mark. Mac users use Command+click. At the default speed of 15 frames per second, this sets up a change that takes place one-third of a second from when the floating box makes its first appearance.

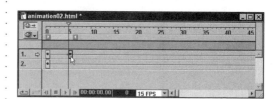

21.

In the Floating Box Inspector, click on the Visible checkbox so that it is deselected. This sets the floating box that's on top to disappear at the specified time.

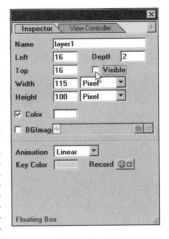

22.

Click on the Loop button at the bottom left side of the Timeline Editor. This sets it up so that the top layer is reset to its original state after it disappears, then becomes invisible again, then resets, and so on for as long as the page is viewed.

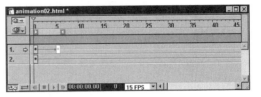

Of course, if you don't want your animation to repeat, skip this step.

23.

Save the file, and then click on the Preview tab to see the animation in action. Adjust the frames per second speed (see Step 10 of Project 1) if desired.

Project 3: Add Actions to a Timeline

This project uses JavaScript actions that, instead of being keyed to standard triggers like having a page load or a visitor click on a link with a mouse, are triggered simply by the passage of a certain amount of time. The animation opens with a moving floating box. When the floating box reaches its destination, the background color changes, and then an image and text are phased in.

1.

Create a Web page named "animation03.html".

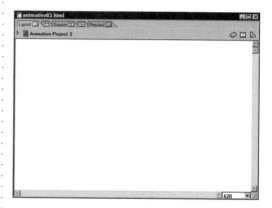

2.

In the Basic tab of the Objects palette, click on the Floating Box icon.

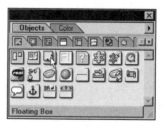

3.

Drag the icon into the Layout Editor and drop it there.

You can also double-click on the icon instead of dragging and dropping it.

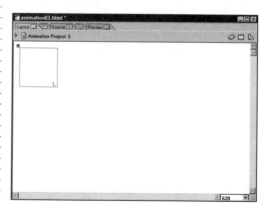

4.

Add two more floating boxes. Drag the new ones aside so that they do not overlap.

5.

Click within the first floating box and type the word "WELCOME" into it.

6.

Select Header 1 from the Paragraph Format drop-down menu in the toolbar, and then click on the Align Center button (the second button to the right of the Paragraph Format menu).

7.

The first floating box expands so that it overlaps the second one. This is not important, because you will be moving the first floating box next.

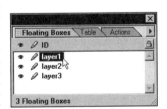

8.

Click on the name of the first floating box in the Floating Boxes palette to select it.

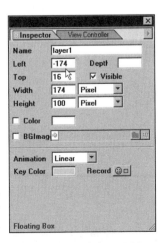

9.

In the Floating Box Inspector, change the value in the Left text box to the same as that in the Width text box, but make it a negative number.

10.

The first floating box is now off screen beyond the left side of the Web page.

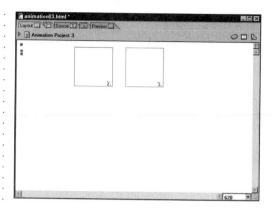

11.

Click on the Image icon in the Objects palette.

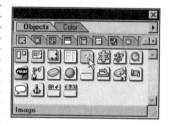

12.

Drag the icon into the second floating box and drop it there.

13.

In the Image Inspector, enter the file name of an image. Alternatively, use either the Point and Shoot button or the Browse button to select an image file.

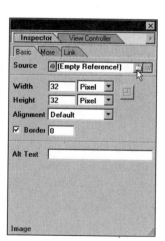

14.

The second floating box expands to accommodate the size of the image; if the image is large enough, the second floating box will overlap the third floating box. Place the mouse pointer over its edge and drag it to the lower center part of the page.

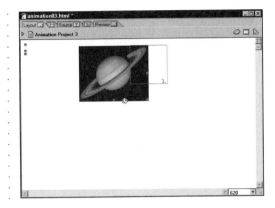

15.

In the Floating Box Inspector, click on the Visible checkbox to deselect it.

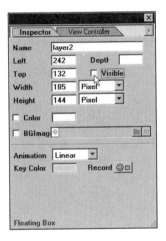

16.

Click within the third floating box and type the word "SATURN" into it.

17.

Select Header 1 from the Paragraph Format drop-down menu in the toolbar.

18.

Highlight the text in the third floating box and click on the Text Color box in the toolbar.

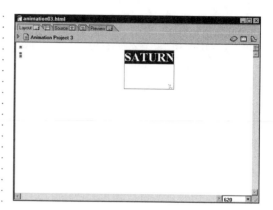

19.

Click on the Named Colors tab in the Color palette.

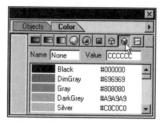

20.

Scroll down the list of colors until you find Cyan, and then click on it to choose it as the text color.

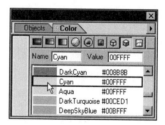

21.

All the elements are now ready for animation, so click on the Timeline Editor button in the toolbar (the one that looks like a filmstrip).

22.

The track for the third floating box is currently selected, because it's the last one that was worked with. Click on the 1 to select the first track instead.

23.

Click on the marker in the first track. This causes the Floating Box Inspector to display the information for the initial position of the first floating box.

24.

In the Floating Box Inspector, select Curve as the animation method.

25.

Ctrl+click on the first track to set up a second marker. Mac users use Command+click.

26.

In the Floating Box Inspector, set the Left and Top coordinates so that the text in the first floating box will end up in the lower right corner of the Web page. In this case, working with GoLive's 620 pixel wide default Layout Area, Left is 440 and Top is 350. You would, of course, need to adjust the numbers to accommodate whatever screen size you are targeting.

27.

In the Timeline Editor, Ctrl+click in the Actions track right above the second animation marker. A question mark will appear.

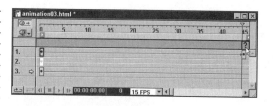

28.

In the Action Inspector, click on the Action button.

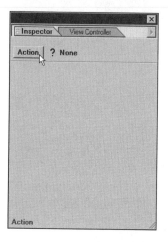

29.

Choose Others|Set BackColor from the menu. This will cause the background color of the Web page to change at the same time as the first floating box comes to rest in the lower right-hand corner.

30.

In the Action Inspector, click on the color box.

31.

In the Named Colors tab of the Color palette, scroll to the top and click on Black to choose it as the background color. This will make the "Welcome" text disappear, incidentally, because it's the same color.

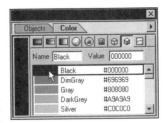

32.

Ctrl+click in the Actions track to the right of the first action. Mac users use Command+click.

Use the scrollbar at the bottom right of the Timeline Editor, if necessary, to get to the right of the first action.

33.

In the Action Inspector, click on the Action button.

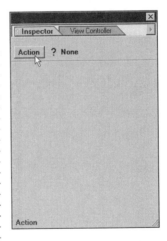

34.

Choose Multimedia|Wipe Transition from the menu. This will be used to fade in the image from the second floating box.

35.

In the Action Inspector, click on the Floating Box arrow and choose layer2 from the drop-down list.

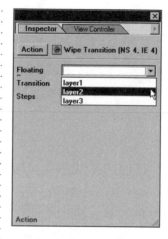

36.

Click on the Transition arrow and choose a transition type from the drop-down list. In this example, we've chosen to use "Wipe Center In," which makes the center of the image appear first, and then expand to show all the image.

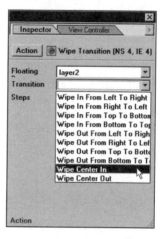

37.

In the Timeline Editor, click on the marker for the third floating box.

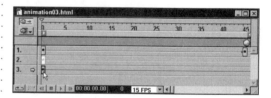

38.

In the Floating Box Inspector, click on the Visible checkbox to deselect it.

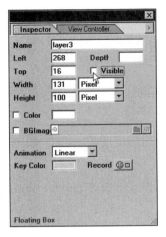

39.

Ctrl+click in the Actions track to the right of the second action. Mac users use Command+click.

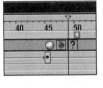

40.

In the Action Inspector, click on the Action button.

Choose Multimedia|Wipe Transition from the menu. This will be used to fade in the text from the third floating box.

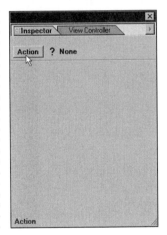

41.

In the Action Inspector, click on the Floating Box arrow and choose layer3 from the drop-down list.

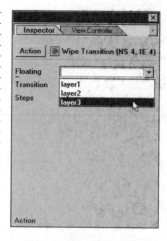

42.

Click on the Transition arrow and choose a transition type from the drop-down list. For the text, we decided to have the left side show up first, and then expand to the right until it's all visible.

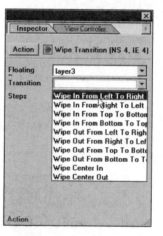

43.

Save the file, and then click on the Preview tab to view the animation.

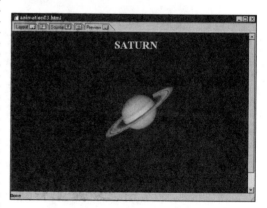

Index

If you like this book, you'll love these...

LOOKING GOOD ON THE WEB
Daniel Gray
ISBN: 1-57610-508-3
224 pages • $29.99 U.S. • $43.99 CANADA

Written from the user's perspective, this book provides a comprehensive, non-technical introduction to Web design. You'll learn how to design and create friendly, easily navigable, award-winning Web sites that please clients and visitors alike.

ILLUSTRATOR® 9 F/X AND DESIGN
Sherry London
ISBN: 1-57610-750-7
560 pages with CD-ROM • $49.99 U.S. • $74.99 CANADA

Features new information and projects on styles and effects, explains how to integrate with Web products, and describes other enhanced features. Using real-world projects, readers learn firsthand how to create intricate illustrations and compositing techniques. Readers also learn how to work seamlessly between Illustrator® and Photoshop®.

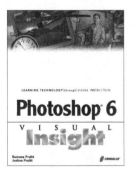

PHOTOSHOP® 6 VISUAL INSIGHT
Ramona Pruitt and Joshua Pruitt
ISBN: 1-57610-747-7
416 pages • $29.99 U.S. • $44.99 CANADA

Learn the basic features of Photoshop®, including layering, masks, and paths, as well as intermediate functions, such as Web graphics, filters, and actions. This book teaches the most useful Photoshop techniques and allows readers to use them in real-world projects, such as repairing images, eliminating red eye, creating type effects, developing Web elements, and more.

ADOBE LIVEMOTION™ VISUAL INSIGHT
Molly Joss
ISBN: 1-57610-787-6
272 pages • $24.99 U.S. • $37.99 CANADA

Examines the fundamentals of LiveMotion™, such as the basic tools and their options. Then it builds on these basics to guide readers through projects that quickly and easily create high-impact, interactive, and animated effects for the Web. Key features described include geometric objects, filters, and the power of styles and layers.

The Coriolis Group, LLC   Telephone: 480.483.0192 • Toll-free: 800.410.0192 • In Canada: 905.477.0722 • www.coriolis.com
Coriolis books are also available at bookstores and computer stores nationwide.